Life and Death Matters

Professionalism and Decision-Making for the First Responder

How paramedics act decisively in the chaos of prehospital emergency medicine

Samuel Adams and Christian Adams
NREMT Paramedics

Twin Peak Publishing, LLC

www.field-medics.com

Info@field-medics.com

ISBN 978-0-9600337-0-6

Life and Death Matters

Professionalism and Decision-Making for the First Responder

Samuel Adams and Christian Adams
NREMT Paramedics

Contents

Section I

The Essential Attributes of a Professional First Responder

1

2

Section II

Building a Framework for Success

3

4

5

6

Introduction: An Integrated Understanding

The primary theme of this book is to develop an integrated understanding of how to operate as a paramedic. These tools go far beyond just operating as a paramedic; they are valuable to any first responder or firefighter.

Three primary qualities must be integrated in order for you to become extremely successful in your work. One is interpersonal skills and personal attributes. Two is decision-making. Three is didactic understanding or educational understanding, which is the knowledge that you gain through all of the study in paramedic school or a fire academy and beyond. Of all three of these, didactic understanding is usually what paramedics spend most of their time on. Operating in emergency situations requires consistent and reliable decisiveness. Didactic understanding does not develop decision-making. Didactic understanding in and of itself does not provide you with the tools to interact with people and build patient rapport. Arguably the most critical aspect of being a paramedic is interpersonal skills in developing a rapport with your patient, with the community, and with your teammates—and then acting decisively.

First and foremost, educational understanding is extremely valuable but must be used and integrated within these two other concepts in order to be properly utilized. It does not benefit your patient, your team, or the community for you to be able to regurgitate information that is not applicable to your current situation or that is over the heads of the patient or your other teammates. If you integrate your education with these other concepts, it will be clearly evident that you know what you are doing.

Didactic understanding and knowledge is beyond the scope of this book. The purpose of this book is to integrate your classroom knowledge (which you have already learned) with two other principles: personal attributes and how to use those attributes to interact with others in emergencies by demonstrating calm and confident decision-making.

A simple analogy will serve to better illustrate why educational information alone does not produce a successful first responder or paramedic. Imagine a house. Imagine how to build a house. You can read all of the books in the world about the different aspects about building a house, from digging a foundation and pouring the concrete, to framing the house and building the different levels within the house. The next step might be to install the plumbing in the house and then run electrical lines to the house. And then finally hanging drywall inside, roofing the house, and putting on the exterior and the interior finishes. You can read a book about every single one of these steps in building a house. Every single one of these tasks is extremely critical in building a stable, habitable house. But reading a book alone on how to do all of these different tasks does not give you the proper tools by which to act.

Eventually you have to make a decision on where you're going to dig the foundation, how you're going to pour the concrete, how you're going to frame the structure. You can only gain this experience and understanding by doing it. The only way to truly become successful is to act and then reflect on the actions that you have taken. Once you have reflected upon the tasks, then you can start to develop, grow, and hone your skills as a homebuilder. And then the educational knowledge from books becomes second nature, and you understand the principles of how you're operating, but now you have a much greater understanding of the overall mission and you are much more capable at building your structure.

But in order to make any of these decisions in the first place, you must have the knowledge, and that takes study and time to develop. In the end, however, the house will never be built if you do not act upon the educational information you have obtained. Another point here is that you cannot watch somebody else build a house and believe that you are now going to be able to build the house the same yourself. If you are not involved in the decision-making of building a house, you will never be able to successfully build one.

Second, interpersonal skills and personal attributes are extremely important for a successful paramedic. You must be able to interact with people. This skill can be learned and developed. Just because it is not inherent in everyone does not mean that you can't learn how to do this. But you must learn by doing—actually building the house. You must remember that you are the professional and that someone has called for your assistance and you have to interact with them. By intentionally building rapport and conscientiously interacting with your patients and with the community, these interpersonal skills will become second nature.

It is critical to understand that we as first responders and paramedics interact with more than just a single patient at a time. We are in a constant state of interacting with the communities we serve at large. By this we mean interacting with witnesses and bystanders at emergency scenes. Interacting with business owners for pre–fire planning and pre–incident planning for possible target hazards. Interacting with the general public during public education workshops or tours. This can also be as simple as interacting with people while shopping for your meals for the shift.

The third concept in this book is decisiveness. You must develop a decision-making process for yourself. You can add to and contribute to your decision-making process the skills that other people have shown you and taught you. But in the end you must have a process that makes sense to you. This is how you will be successful and how you will be able to act decisively.

We discuss these three concepts in this book. However, understand that the first principle of educational knowledge cannot be fully elaborated on within this book. We stated earlier that it is beyond the scope of this book, but it is our intention to provide you with an understanding of how to integrate your knowledge with the two other main principles. Educational understanding is discussed to some degree, but it is discussed because it is integrated with the other two principles. You cannot have one without the other two. We do not intend to replace or provide you with medical knowledge. That knowledge must be attained through continuing education.

These three concepts used in an integrated fashion will greatly enhance your ability as a paramedic. You will gain a better understanding of the overall objective that we as paramedics, first responders, and firefighters are attempting to accomplish, and you will know how to better serve the community that you are now working in.

In order to develop a sound decision-making process, you have to integrate all these skills. Develop them all individually so they can be useful as one tool.

We want to make something clear. A paycheck is not what makes you a professional. Professionalism is the internal embodiment of how you conduct yourself. To all the volunteers out there, keep up the good work! Keep going out the door. Your selfless sacrifice to your communities is invaluable.

Section I

The Essential Attributes of a Professional First Responder

1

The Character of a First Responder

What are the key attributes or characteristics a paramedic should have to be successful? The job of a paramedic is not just medicine; it is much more difficult than understanding basic medical principles. An integrated understanding of medicine, personal interaction, and personal character attributes will help you grow as a paramedic and will give you the ability to teach others more efficiently.

Throughout this section we will explore the attributes that are key to providing successful and professional prehospital care. This is not an exhaustive list, but it is a starting point on how and why you conduct yourself as a professional. These individual attributes can be categorized into the three principles of medicine, interpersonal skills, and personal attributes. It is critical to your success as a paramedic to integrate these three principles into your practice.

An integrated understanding of these principles is absolutely essential. For example, your personal attribute of integrity will directly impact your ability to have effective personal interactions, which will then directly impact your medicine. Because of the integrated understanding that we are developing in the paramedic, some of these attributes are found in more than just one of the principles set forth.

Humility

Sincere humility is one of the most important attributes a paramedic must exhibit. However, this trait can be difficult for certain individuals because they believe they have sincere humility, but internally they express fake humility. Fake humility is maybe one of the most dangerous attributes that someone can exhibit. Fake humility is destructive to your ability to apply what you know to properly treat someone. Fake humility is also dangerous in your personal life, because it never allows you to develop and grow. This is dangerous because fake humility is lip service. In practice, you sit and listen to constructive criticism respectfully, but in your prideful arrogance, you do not consider what someone might be saying to you.

To better illustrate fake humility, here's a simple and far-too-common example. Paramedic A is on scene and implementing an appropriate treatment plan. Paramedic B arrives on scene and is brought up to speed on what is going on with the patient and what the treatment plan is. Paramedic A has already developed a plan of action to transport the patient to the hospital and has initiated all of the proper interventions. Paramedic B then states that they want to do something differently. Paramedic A states they have already initiated this plan and are moving toward the hospital. Paramedic B then says okay, sounds good, and appears to be humble and recognize that a plan has already been initiated that is completely appropriate for the patient. Then, however, paramedic B does not help implement the plan and, instead, undermines the treatment plan in place. This is fake humility. Paramedic B is not humble enough to recognize someone else has implemented an appropriate plan and does not fully help to implement it as a team member.

True humility is such a key attribute for growth because it requires you to understand that there's always more to learn. Because there are many avenues to learn new information, you have to be open to all of them—whether it's taking new classes for education, reading, personal study, or other people's constructive criticism. You have to be open to other people and their ideas. True humility allows you the freedom and liberty to openly discuss new ideas and techniques.

This attribute is important to new paramedic development. If you're a new paramedic, it is dangerous for you to believe that you have full understanding of all the different aspects of all the different calls you go on. The EMS system and the fire service in the United States and internationally are now so dynamic that you can never know everything. We would argue that you will never know everything despite how long you have been serving. You have to be open to new and better ways of doing what you do every day.

Humility allows personal growth. Without personal growth you will continue to treat people the same way that you always have. You will never allow yourself the ability to develop new ways of treatment for patients without humility. We will let you in on a secret: You don't know everything. And you certainly will always have room to grow. Recognizing that you don't know everything is the foundation that needs to be laid in order for your success to take place. The quicker you embrace the fact that you will never know everything, which should drive you toward self-growth and professionalism, the better off you will be. The vehicle to do this is humility.

Now don't misunderstand. Being humble should not hinder your ability to act in critical situations or on regular noncritical calls. Humility, on the other hand, should actually increase your ability to intervene and act. If you approach your work with the understanding that there may be something going on that you don't fully understand, that you are not fully aware of, such awareness gives you more ability and mentality to treat the situation seriously. And by the time you get to the emergency room, their symptoms may have resolved, or you might have reversed whatever was causing the patient's ailment. By being aggressive in the first place and having the understanding that you need to be aggressive and that things could get much worse, you stayed in front of the patient's decline.

One of the other key features of humility is that it allows you to continue searching for other problems with your patient. It requires you to continue to have ongoing assessments. It allows you to see that there is sometimes more than one disease process taking place with somebody. Humility requires that you, the paramedic, continue to search for other problems that might crop up during the patient care. Your assessment should never be complete until you pull in and drop the patient off at the emergency room, and we would argue care still doesn't end there. Learning continues to take place.

The learning that we're speaking of is follow-up information with the patient to see if you were going down the right track. Humility is a touchy thing, and most people understand that they should strive for it. Most people will tell you that they have humility, but in their head they are in a constant state of frustration and belief that they're right all the time. This is demonstrative of fake humility. This is a dangerous place to be because it doesn't allow for outside input and follow-up information to be applied.

Humility is a characteristic that people do understand they should have or should practice. In some way humility can be practiced and developed. In order to do so, you have to understand where it really comes from. Humility is a state of mind or an attitude. It is recognition of your own flaws and imperfections. If you practice and run your calls in a way that you are always trying to learn something new from a call—and you are in a constant state of practicing reflection and self-reflection and trying to learn from the different patients that you have—this will help develop your humility. You realize that you don't know everything. And the more that you consciously develop humility, the more you recognize how little you really do know and the more understanding you gain.

Practicing humility gives you the ability to act and intervene on critical patients. Your confidence increases because you understand that you need to stay in front of the game, so that if the patient does collapse on you, you have systems in place that allow you to more easily treat that patient. Because you practice humility, you anticipate a patient's inevitable decline. As a new paramedic, or even as a seasoned paramedic, you should never assume you know everything.

Ego or Pride

On every single call you go on as a new paramedic or a seasoned paramedic, you better be checking your ego at the door. Ego is perhaps the most dangerous personal character attribute of a paramedic. Emergency medicine has no room for your ego. New paramedics and their egos and seasoned paramedics and their egos are extremely detrimental to a patient.

Your ego inhibits your ability to treat your patients. Your ego inhibits your ability to act. You cannot approach your calls with the understanding that you always know what's going on. We'll reveal another secret here: It's okay not to know exactly what's going on. In fact, one could argue that it's better to have a more global picture than to get caught with a narrow view of what's going on with your patient. It is not the paramedic's job to specifically diagnose somebody with a certain disease process. It is your job to recognize life threats and recognize what you might be able to do to intervene.

Integrity

Integrity is a quality that each individual should always be striving to achieve. Integrity is elusive. Every individual is always tested and tempted with the easy way out, whether that's in work or life. Integrity can have many different facets, such as discipline, accountability, and honesty. And the idea is that we have to constantly strive for it and implement it. There are so many different ways to define what this word means, but everyone has a general understanding of what integrity embodies. A short definition of this word might look something like this: to do what is right even when no one is looking.

Integrity is difficult to attain because, in order to attain it, you have to conscientiously think about it. You have to will yourself in order to achieve integrity. Integrity is ever elusive and must be on your mind as often as possible. You must discipline your life to maintain your integrity. Practicing integrity must become habitual; then it will become subconscious. The constant act of having integrity will become easier the more you practice.

In your work and in your life as a paramedic, integrity plays an incredibly key role. You must always be on the alert for situations that will arise for you to take the easy way out. One of the biggest ways that this will manifest itself is usually in workload. The simple example of this is running a multicar traffic accident with multiple victims and your determining that some are not patients because of minor injuries. Now, instead of doing assessments and refusals on these patients, you take the easy way out and assume that they will be okay. This is an example of taking the easy way out. There can be major consequences for having this sort of thinking. Your patient may very well have a serious injury or be on the verge of a serious injury. You might miss a fractured cervical spine or internal bleeding that the hospital would have found if they were transported.

Integrity is vital to the paramedic. You have to practice it on almost every call you go on. Think about what we really do: going into people's houses and into their bedrooms with absolute trust from the patient and the family members. The public trusts you, and trusts that you're there to help, that you are not there to take advantage of them. Your integrity is what builds a relationship with each patient that you come in contact with. You will be asked many times to go get a patient's wallet, or to get their keys or to lock their doors. It's imperative that you do this with the utmost integrity.

You are not only doing this for yourself, but the way you conduct yourself will affect every single paramedic in the country. Be professional! Your actions can have ripple effects and cause the public to lose trust in the system we have in place to help them in emergencies. Do what's right because it is right. If you're not doing that, why are you in this job?

Integrity filters down to more than just the patients that you interact with. Your business or your employer is trusting you with thousands and in some cases millions of dollars' worth of equipment. You have to maintain this equipment; you have to use it appropriately and check it and make sure it's in good working order. You have to report errors and mistakes. In doing so, you build integrity. Instill trust with your employer, instill trust with your patient, and instill trust with your team.

You will always accomplish more *with* your team than without them. Your teammates must trust you, and they must know that you as the paramedic are looking out for their well-being. This is demonstrated by how you treat and how you act around your patients. How you interact with the public is on display every single day. Your teammates can see clearly whether or not you conduct yourself with integrity and whether or not you're consistent with it.

Compassion

Compassion is a natural attribute that all good paramedics must have. Compassion is much more than just merely caring about the victims and patients that you will attend. You should have a genuine desire to help those in need. It's not enough to say that you care about them. It's not enough to say that you just want to help. Why did you get into this job? You need to reflect on this question and come to an answer that you can fully articulate. It can't be a cookie-cutter answer.

Compassion, however, can be difficult at times. We all run calls that will stress and challenge you. In order to achieve real success at being a paramedic, you must have true compassion. You have to truly care about the people that you are helping. You have to care about the grandmother or grandfather that you're helping up off the ground at two o'clock in the morning. You have to care about the situation that the homeless find themselves in—even though these situations can stress us and bring us to our breaking point. You must maintain your compassion in order to fully and more completely treat people. It will make you a better paramedic and a better person.

Someone we know, who is no longer with us, sums up compassion eloquently: You are not better than anybody, but you might be better off. This statement truly embodies and defines what compassion is for the paramedic, and not just the medic but for you and your fellow man. You must come to the understanding that you are not intrinsically more valuable than anybody else. Every single person has the same intrinsic value, but due to circumstances and situations in social settings, some individuals find themselves in difficult circumstances. In order to truly care for these people, you have to understand that you are not better than they are, but you may be better off. If you approach being a paramedic with this mentality, it will serve you well.

One of the first skills that we learn as EMS providers is called patient care. Patient care is a broad term for all of the assessment, interventions, and transport that the paramedic has involvement with. Patient care is what every good paramedic should strive to perfect. You will never achieve perfection in this, but that doesn't mean that you can't try. The second word of this phrase is *care*. If you do not care about your patient, then why are you here? If you do not care about what happens to your patient, it will negatively impact your patient care. Having genuine compassion for the care you provide and caring about what happens to your patients and what happens to your victims is important, and such qualities will drive you to take better care of them. Make no mistake, this can be clearly seen and interpreted by your patient, victims, and your teammates.

Here we come again to this idea of teammates. The team. Your team will see if you have compassion, which is directly related to how you treat people. If you don't treat people well and you don't treat people with care and compassion, then what confidence does your team have that you are looking out for them? If you do not demonstrate compassion with the people that you treat, it will affect your relationship with your team. This will affect how much your team trusts you and how much they can rely on you.

The collaboration with EMS, the fire service, and police departments is perhaps the greatest display of teamwork on the planet. You as the paramedic play an integral role in that team. You can demonstrate to this team how you care about them by taking care of your fellow man in their time of need. This attribute is contagious, and team members will respond appropriately and will be encouraged by your compassion.

Empathy

Another key element that must be factored in for life and for patient care is empathy. Try to understand where your patient is coming from and try to understand and be empathetic to their situation. You must be sensitive to the situations that your patients find themselves in. Even though you might not have an emotional stake in a given situation, you have to be sensitive to it.

People can tell when you don't care. People can tell when you are just going through the motions. We're not going to lie to you and tell you that we're always empathetic because we're not, but this is something that we should all strive for. Try to be aware of the circumstances that some of these people will call you for. This can be difficult, but a judgmental attitude will not bode well for your career.

This attribute of empathy goes hand-in-hand with caring for people. Just take care of your patient. Why did you become a paramedic if you don't care? Be sensitive and understanding of where people are with life circumstances, the different disease processes that you see, and the different levels of trauma. Be understanding and empathetic toward your patient. Do you think so highly of yourself to believe that you're never going to be in the situation that some of these people are in? Or that you'll never be in a traffic accident, or you will never have cancer, or you will never have a GI bleed, or you will never be homeless? Do you really think that highly of yourself? Take the time to empathize with your patient's situation and take care of them.

Your team will recognize if you are empathetic with people or not. Why would your team think that you would be empathetic with them if you are in a constant state of judgment toward others? We all have struggles that we deal with in our lives and need help with. Your teammates need to know that you won't judge them and you will be there for them. This is demonstrated by being consistently compassionate and empathetic with your patients.

What Drives You?

What drives you? For some of us this is an easy question to answer, but other people struggle with the answer. You have to get past the cliché of "we want to help people." Of course you become a paramedic because you want to help people. The problem is that this answer will leave you lacking. This answer will not sustain you when you become tired and rundown.

After years of paramedicine, you can become jaded and forget why you're doing this in the first place. You should try to develop a deeper reason and a deeper understanding of why you really went to paramedic school. Everybody must do this on their own. It starts with wanting to help people, of course. But you need to elaborate. You need to try to come to a better understanding of what drives you. The answer will motivate you to become better. If you have a better understanding of why you became a paramedic, you'll find it self-motivating.

Self-motivation is extremely important because this is what will drive you to be better. When you get burned out or tired or don't want to study anymore, your answer will be there to sustain you. The way to develop self-motivation is to understand why you chose to do this work in the first place. For some people this answer is going to be more pay, more opportunities, more benefits, or even a larger scope of practice. You should take the time to try to understand why you're doing this. It doesn't have to be complex, but you should be able to articulate your thoughts so that you can hold onto and rely on your self-motivation.

If you became a paramedic or first responder because you think it's cool or you saw something on TV that motivated you briefly, or you wanted to get a cool T-shirt, these reasons will leave you quickly. They will not sustain you and will not motivate you to grow. A TV paramedic and a T-shirt paramedic don't do the public any good. This type of motivation is fleeing from you; you have to have something that's more tangible. You have to want to serve people.

Accountability and Responsibility

Personal accountability is a fundamental attribute to being a paramedic or first responder. Professionalism is not about whether you get paid; it is about how you conduct yourself. Accountability is integral to the professional. In the role of paramedic you have an enormous responsibility, and you will be held accountable for it. You are accountable to yourself, your team, and the public. The personal attribute of accountability assumes that you will acknowledge and take responsibility for your actions and decisions.

Accountability as an attribute can be discussed and defined for days. We can begin to address the principles of accountability as they relate to your profession as a paramedic or first responder and yet never fully articulate the importance of it. Accountability, we believe, begins first and foremost with *you*. You must hold yourself accountable for the actions you take and for what you say. But what does this really mean? How do you hold yourself accountable?

Being able to hold yourself accountable is a direct reflection of your personal integrity. And your personal integrity is a direct reflection of your professionalism. Make no mistake about it, true professionals have integrity and, as such, will hold themselves accountable for their actions. In the world of paramedicine, if you don't hold yourself accountable for what you do, for the way you treat people, and for interventions that you perform, you are not a true professional. This is your first priority. You must begin holding yourself accountable, which will result in true professionalism and will be evident among your peers and employer. But more than that, it will be evident to you. Personal accountability is the key. With it you have ascended to be a professional paramedic.

Your holding yourself accountable is contagious. When you are so willing to be accountable and take ownership for what you do, others quickly follow suit. You now have created an environment in which your actions and your treatment of people are completely trusted because there are no insidious intentions or cavalier decisions. Your teammates will now hold themselves accountable to you and others. The people you work with will immediately understand that your actions are purposeful and intentional, with nothing but the patient's best interest in mind.

The other important issue here is that when you hold yourself accountable for what you do and the interventions you perform, you have gained the utmost trust from your medical directors. They will loosen the reins, so to speak, on your patient care because they understand that, if something happens, you will address it with them. There is no longer any mistrust because you will always hold yourself to the standard of care.

This is what personal accountability is. It's the principle that you yourself will take responsibility when asked, but, more than that, you will freely admit and bring attention to items when you know you've made a mistake. It's taking responsibility and acknowledging that you have made an error. True personal accountability doesn't only pertain to those aspects discovered by your willingness to omit certain facts from a narrative or patient care story. You can't omit certain details from ient care report or discussion and believe this is being able. It's more than acknowledging a mistake when it's brought to you; it's that act of actually bringing the mistake forward yourself.

Having personal accountability also creates an environment of liberty. When you are so willing to fall on the sword with accountability for what you do, you have free liberty to act. This is directly related to your decision-making and your ability to act as it relates to the professional. When you have true liberty as a result of your personal accountability, your patient care will improve enormously. Your thoughts are no longer on what actions you should or shouldn't be doing; they are on what is in the best interest of your patient.

You will now be making decisions based on patient care rather than on fear for what the implications of your decisions may be. Your ability to make decisions is directly related to your willingness to be responsible for the decisions you make. When you operate in an environment of fear, you are paralyzed. Don't act in fear; act in liberty. With liberty comes ability to act.

We want to briefly mention the idea of obligation as it relates to accountability. As paramedics and first responders, we have to understand that we are obligated to treat people and act in their best interests. We have an obligation to be a patient advocate. This obligation is not merely a term but a binding principle of a paramedic in general. That obligation creates an environment in which you are responsible for that patient. You must understand that you are responsible for how you treat the patient that you are obligated to provide care for. By understanding that principle, you must take accountability for how you treat them. This may be a little difficult, but we don't want it to become convoluted. You are obligated to treat people. You are responsible for the treatment that you render these people. You then must hold yourself accountable for the treatment you performed.

You not only have to embody the characteristic of personal accountability, you also have to demonstrate that you are accountable to your team. Your team can be anybody from your EMT partner, your paramedic partner, your fire department crew, to any environment in which you find yourself providing prehospital care. If your team doesn't understand that you will hold yourself accountable for your decisions, they won't trust you. Also, if you're not accountable to your team, they have no confidence in your willingness to put them first. If you don't hold yourself accountable to your team, they won't have any confidence that you're properly training them, that you're properly instructing them, and that you're properly advising them on patient care.

Finally, you're accountable to the public. Make no mistake: We as paramedics, firefighters, and first responders are servants of the public. We signed up taking oaths to defend the public, to serve the public, and volunteered to respond to their emergencies. You are accountable to them. What does this mean? You're accountable for how you conduct yourself privately inside the fire station. Are you wasting your time or are you diligently training? Are you conducting yourself in a way that the public would be proud to say that you respond to their emergency? You're accountable to the public for how you conduct yourself in public. You're accountable for how you interact with the community on a nonemergent level, whether you're in the fire station or in the grocery store. They will hold you accountable for what you do, and you should hold yourself accountable for how you interact with them. Be a professional.

Personal accountability also gives you control of your response to your employer or supervisor, if or when you are disciplined. When you admit fault, your supervisors no longer feel the need to question your integrity. Admitting will lower your risk in relation to your job or position, because you accept responsibilities for your actions. You create an environment where you participate in your own disciplinary action. What you do impacts your professional life, not your boss or supervisor or anyone else, YOU! Like we said before, the immediate result of personal accountability is personal liberty.

Holding yourself accountable is actually very simple in concept but can be difficult in practice. In principle what does this mean? Simply that you will take responsibility for your actions, and you will hold yourself accountable. You will not shy away from the decisions that were questionable or statements that were made incorrectly. You will not only hold yourself accountable when addressed with difficult questions, you will freely offer yourself and admit when you have made a mistake. This is important, because not only do you admit the mistake when asked, you actually bring attention to it.

You're responsible for maintaining your team's training and maintaining their skill set and knowledge. You're responsible for developing them as a team in order to be as effective as possible. You're responsible now for a large amount of equipment and medications including controlled substances. These responsibilities should not be taken lightly. You are also responsible for your continuing education and making sure that you maintain all your requirements by your department or agency. You are accountable to your medical director and medical division. You have to stay current on your protocols and your guidelines, and you are going to be held accountable if you do something outside of your scope of practice or breach your protocols.

The largest area that you're responsible for, however, is providing the standard of care for your patients. Now you have the obligation to intervene for people when they can't intervene for themselves. This is a huge responsibility that you will be held accountable for. You're going to be faced with people who don't want your help and are adamant about not receiving it; however, they may not be capable of refusing it. You're going to be running on people who have altered mental status, and they're not going to be able to think clearly about what's going on. You're going to have to intervene for these people, and you're obligated to do so.

You're now responsible for making decisions so that people receive the definitive care they need. You're responsible for making sure that your specific patients go to the hospital that is most appropriate for them. You're responsible to know what conditions the hospitals in your system are able to accommodate, and what they're not able to accommodate, and why certain people need to go to certain hospitals. In many circumstances you are responsible for starting a patient's overall medical care.

More and more today, you will now be responsible for people's primary care. Citizens are going to call 911 to be evaluated and checked out and are going to want your opinion on what afflicts them. You're going to be responsible to give them the best information that you can and make the decisions for their overall medical care. You are their primary way of getting to the hospital to receive the emergency care and their primary care. You're now responsible to provide the standard of care for all the people that you treat.

For every single patient that you interact with, you're now responsible to make sure that they are okay, and if they need help, they receive the definitive care they need. Whether or not you believe it's an emergency is irrelevant. Your idea of an emergency is not necessarily the patient's idea of an emergency. You are now responsible for taking care of these people.

Ownership and Professionalism

These two words sum up everything we have covered. These two words should be ingrained into your ideology of how to come to work every day, and the mentality that you should strive for. Everyone will fall short of maintaining these concepts all the time, but consciously thinking of these two words will serve you well.

You are going to make mistakes. There are far too many variables and situations that you will get into to maintain perfection. The key, however, is to take ownership when you make a mistake and take action to learn from it. Do not fear making mistakes. Use them as learning opportunities, and you will quickly make fewer. The beautiful thing about ownership and professionalism is that they are contagious. When you conduct yourself with a professional attitude toward your department or agency, your engine, truck, or ambulance and maintain your equipment and make sure it is in good working order, your team will see. If you practice professionalism with the easier things like the engine and truck, it will bleed over and become natural with your patient care. You have to be a professional because the people you serve are relying on you to be. For many of you, they are paying for it with their tax money.

The funny part about ownership and professionalism is that most of us understand the concepts intellectually and can see their value from that aspect. Yet few of us actually implement them into our lives. Fewer still are able to maintain and be consistent; however, practice and conscious action and execution will build sound habits. When your team sees your actions and how you conduct yourself with ownership and professionalism, you are silently giving them the liberty and encouragement to do the same. If you take ownership of what happens with your equipment and rigs, and with your patients, the public will see it too. Your patients can pick up on the subtle gentleness and professionalism that you can provide for them when they are in need.

Some of the greatest joy will come from the simplest of calls if you conduct yourself as a professional. Be a professional, own your mistakes, and own the decisions you make.

The biggest part of this, however, is to remember to remain professional for yourself—even if it does not filter to the rest of your team. These two ideas will be the softest pillow that you can have as an emergency responder. They will drive you to do your best and clear your conscience when you doubt yourself. Make no mistake, sooner or later you will doubt yourself and be upset with yourself about a treatment or intervention, but a professional attitude and ownership of what you have done will get you through it.

Decision-Making

Decision-making is the key to everything you will do as a paramedic. That's why decision-making is perhaps the most important personal character attribute of developing a new paramedic. This can also be characterized as a personal interaction attribute. Decision-making is all about how to decide what to do with the information that you have. Decision-making will be covered at length in chapter 6.

Intent

What is intent? Do you live your life with intent? Do you wake up in the morning with intent? Do you approach being a medic or first responder with intent? Do you make decisions with clear intention behind them? Do you make decisions with the potential consequences in mind? Do you take into account what will happen given the decisions that you make? Do you conduct yourself with intent? Intention is decisiveness with purpose.

These are all questions that you should wrestle with. You should analyze each one of these questions and come to a conclusion about them. Don't take the easy way out and make up some cookbook answer. You need to be able to articulate what you are intending to accomplish. You need to be clear minded. If you don't take the time to try to understand what your intentions are, your goals become much more difficult to attain. Intention is one of the key aspects of attaining your goals. You have to articulate what you want. You have to be able to take into account foreseeable consequences and side effects and must be able to anticipate what your actions produce.

To act with intention is extremely important for the paramedic. It allows you to anticipate needs and problems that might arise. It causes you to be more active than passive. If you attack a problem and have aggressive treatment, you are no longer solely reacting to the situation. A simple example would be a trauma patient that is bleeding from the leg. You apply direct pressure and pack the wound, but it continues to bleed. Just stop the bleeding. Put a tourniquet on it and stop the bleeding. Your intention is to stop the bleeding, so stop it, instead of continuing to react to your patient still bleeding.

Moving with intention and decision-making with intention is critical. Intention is also important because it forces you to own a decision that you're making. If you are decisive and accountable with what you are doing, you will have more confidence.

You have to approach every single call with the intention of making situations better for the victim or patient that you encounter. You have to treat them with the intention of making their lives better for having met you. You cannot have a cavalier attitude with the intention of just getting to the call so that you can get to the next one. There is always another call, so treat the one that you are on with clear intention of making it better for the patient you're with.

Refuse to step out of your engine, truck, or ambulance with a casual attitude. You have to move with intention in order to mitigate the emergency. You cannot be casual about your approach. If you are casual, it's not you who is going to suffer but the citizens. Like we talked about before, if you don't care about what you are doing, then why are you here? Again be a professional.

These traits make up the character of a first responder. Now we'll discuss the essential interpersonal skills first responders need, along with these character traits.

2

Essential Interpersonal Skills

Interpersonal skills are extremely important to the paramedic. Patient care revolves around the ability to interact effectively with others. Of course your education will drive decisions for patient care, but if you develop interpersonal skills, you will be much more effective in your job. This chapter builds a basic foundation for interpersonal skills to develop and then integrate into your practice.

General and Self-Reflection

General reflection and self-reflection are two of the most effective ways for a new paramedic to develop growth. Paramedics should be in a constant state of reflection. Reflection allows you to analyze the situation with intent.

There are two types of reflection. Self-reflection, which is you as an individual reflecting on how you reacted to the situation and what took place. Then general reflection, which is trying to analyze the overall picture or situation. What was the situation? Was it a cardiac arrest, a difficulty breathing, a sick cardiac patient, a septic patient? Reflection in general allows you to better analyze the patient and better analyze the situation you were in.

Self-reflection, as mentioned earlier, is the ability and the time you take to understand how you reacted to a situation. Both self-reflection and general reflection are so important to your development and growth, particularly for a new paramedic, because these skills give you the opportunity to see where you are and what you need to develop. With them, you have the ability to understand what areas you are deficient in, and what you need to do in order to overcome those deficiencies.

General reflection is important because it allows you to break down the individual call or situation that you've been on. It allows you to analyze the different medications used and the different treatments and interventions that you might have initiated. General reflection gives you the ability to chalk away calls in your personal rolodex so that when you see the situation again, you are better able to recall the event. You then have a better understanding of what might be going on and have a sharper ability to anticipate what may take place.

By doing this general reflection on all of your calls, especially as a new paramedic, it builds your frame of reference faster. General reflection is important because it allows you to understand medication dosages, procedures, treatment plans in general, and how to treat someone. It also develops an idea of intent (discussed in the last chapter)—it gives you intention for what you want to work on.

Personal reflection, we believe, is much more valuable. Self-reflection on how you relate to a call is important because you have to understand why *you* did what you did. Self-reflection gives you the time and the intention of trying to develop your decision-making skills. Self-reflection allows you to try to analyze why you reacted in certain situations the way that you did, and that is extremely important. Self-reflection is how you develop a decision-making process and a consistent method by which to treat patients. Self-reflection also allows you to identify areas in your character that are lacking.

Personal reflection can be difficult, and you have to be honest with yourself. Self-reflection goes hand-in-hand with humility. You have to approach the process from all angles especially if you want to get the most out of the lesson learned. You want to gain a better understanding of what's going on, and you want to gain a better understanding of how you react to certain situations, and you want to get a better understanding of your character flaws that you need to overcome. Personal reflection is going to be a career-long process.

Why and how you react to situations is going to change throughout your career based on your experience, and that's going to cause you to become more comfortable. However, the personal reflection can't stop when you become comfortable. In fact, self-reflection becomes even more important. With comfort comes complacency. You have to be in a constant state of self-reflection so that you don't lose your edge. There are plenty of times that you are going to feel as if you don't know what's going on, and self-reflection will help you through that. Self-reflection allows the seasoned paramedic to recognize when they're becoming too cavalier and not showing the proper amount of compassion and empathy for the patients they are treating.

Teamwork

Teamwork. There's so much to be said about teamwork. Everything you do in emergency situations revolves around teamwork. Teamwork requires constant attention to both your interpersonal skills and personal attributes. Teamwork will also directly affect how successful you are at practicing prehospital medicine. Every single person has a role to play. Everybody brings traits to the table that can be utilized.

Teamwork starts with developing yourself first. And then you have to take the responsibility of developing your own people. You have to develop your partner, and you have to develop your fellow firefighters on the engine or the truck. You cannot hoard information because you as the paramedic believe that you have more knowledge and understanding than the rest of your team. You have to take the time to invest in your crew and take the time to develop their own understanding of what's going on with certain calls.

The better your crew understands what your needs are and what you're thinking, the better they will be at anticipating what you're going to need. Even more important than anticipating what you're going to need, they will pick up on things that you miss. If you develop a good team, when you miss something, they are going to support you, and you are going to be able to rely on them just as much as they rely on you. You are going to miss things. Without a good team behind you, you're going to fall flat on your face. Developing a team is one of the most important tasks you should do as a paramedic. You have to invest in your crew just as much as you invest in yourself. You have to involve them in what is going on. You have to involve them in all aspects of patient care.

Your crew members are going to have different skill sets and different ideas and ways of addressing certain situations that you come across. The more diverse a group of people you have around you, the stronger it will make you. Everybody lacks in certain areas, and your team can help you when you are struggling. That's not going to happen if you don't develop a collegial working relationship with your crew and develop your team. If you take the time to develop your team, they will be able to recognize when you are deviating from your normal methodology. They can address a situation if something abnormal is taking place. It will be obvious to them that you're doing something different.

Doing something different is perfectly acceptable; however, it is reassuring to have teammates recognize that you are doing something different. This reduces the instances of you as the medic overlooking something. It's good to have somebody to look out for you and to be able to inform you: *Hey, are you sure this is what you want to do? Are you sure this is the route that you want to take? You know you normally don't do this, right?* Your teammates' ability to look out for you and for the patient can only happen if you develop a team.

Communication

Communication is integral to every single action you take as a paramedic. Think about how much communication takes place on a single call: Someone calls 911 and communicates with dispatch. Dispatch communicates with you. The patient communicates with you about what is going on. You communicate with your team about what your plan is and how to implement it. You communicate with the patient about what you are doing and what you are seeing. You communicate with the hospital about your thoughts and what the incoming patient has going on.

Communication as a skill set can be developed and practiced. Communication is vitally important. Working in emergency settings is stressful. Because your work is stressful, communication becomes even that much more important. You must intentionally and actively communicate with your teammates. If you fail to communicate with your teammates about what needs to happen with a critical patient, that inaction will absolutely affect patient care. Not only can it affect patient care, but it can compromise your safety. If you see something, say something.

When we think about communication, one thought immediately comes to mind. To illustrate the importance of communication, we impress upon you one fact. The National Institute for Occupational Safety and Health (NIOSH) five are the five factors that are known to play a role in almost every single firefighter injury or death on a fireground. One of the NIOSH five is a *lack of communication*. Communication has a direct impact on the success of a call. It is directly related to scene presence and setting the tone as the leader of an emergency medical or trauma team. Communication is integral no matter where you fit in the command structure of all incidents, including MCIs or large traffic accidents.

We cannot stress enough how important communication is—both for providing outstanding patient care and for you and your team's safety.

Set the Tone

When someone calls 911 for an emergency—and we mean a true emergency—you're always beginning behind the eight ball. When you walk in the door as a paramedic, you have to understand that you're walking into the unknown. You're walking into a chaotic situation that somehow you have to make sense of. The others in the room including your crew members, the patient, the family, witnesses, and other agencies are going to stand there and look at what you're going to do. All eyes are on you.

Now it's time to put you to the test. Are you able to rise to the challenge? Are you able to really put to good use what you've learned in school? This isn't the time to learn how to read an EKG. This isn't the time to study your dosages for specific drugs. This isn't the time to figure out how to turn the monitor on or what the defibrillator button does. This is the time to act. This is the time to make decisions. This is the time to instill confidence. This is the time to set the tone.

The first five minutes of a call can make or break it—and make all the difference in the world, both good and bad. It's incredibly important to instill confidence in the patient, family, bystanders on scene, and your fellow teammates or crew members. You can do this by setting the proper tone.

By setting the proper tone, everything begins to slow down, and you're able to more effectively communicate to your teammates. You're more effectively going to be able to communicate to the patient, the patient's family, and all the bystanders. You are more effective in every way by setting a proper and confident tone.

If you walk in the door and you do not set the tone of leadership, leadership will arise, somebody else will take over, and somebody else will start making decisions. But that's not their responsibility; it's yours. You have to be the one to set the tone.

By setting the proper tone, you can now more quickly analyze the situation. You can determine quicker what your differential diagnoses are, what the proper treatment plan is, figure out how to more effectively and efficiently implement that treatment plan, and most importantly reassess the patient and reassess the treatment.

You have to be able to take what is chaotic and make sense of it. You are expected to put the pieces together and form a plan. You have to be decisive in your actions, and you must effectively communicate to all the other people involved. All of these actions are included in setting the tone.

Let us use a respiratory call to demonstrate setting the proper tone. You walk in the door to a sick respiratory patient who is on the verge of respiratory failure. You assert yourself as the paramedic running the call, immediately assess the patient's breathing status, and then decisively start to communicate a treatment plan. You set the tone with command presence, certainty of action, and confidence in your treatment plan. Your decisiveness and clear communication to your teammates sets the proper tone and demonstrates to the patient and your team that you are intervening with confidence.

On the other side of this, if you walk in the door and are timid and shy about physical assessment and lack confidence in your physical exam, it then affects your decision-making. Your decisions are no longer made confidently, and you are worried about making the right choice. You look around for input and try to find someone to validate what you think you might want to do. You are not treating the patient confidently and intervening with certainty. Your tone now demonstrates uncertainty, and the scene can quickly spiral out of control on a patient who is truly sick.

And let's be clear. Setting a proper tone doesn't mean standing there stoically as if whatever you're confronted with isn't affecting you or doesn't bother you in the least bit. Setting the proper tone means taking action in spite of what you're confronted with, in spite of what you're faced with. Take action decisively in order to properly mitigate the problem, treat the patient, and figure out the solution to solve the problem.

Next time you're on a call or running an alarm, take a look at the paramedic running the call to see how the tone is set. When the medic starts to get nervous, you can see the anxiety rise in the room. You can see the anxiety rise in everybody around including the patient, the family members, and the fellow crew members.

The anxiety certainly rises when the anxiety of the paramedic rises. You have to be the calmest and coolest in the room and able to make the best decisions. You can't make decisions based on an emotional response to what is unfolding in front of you.

You have to be able to evaluate the information and make a proper decision.

By setting a proper tone, you begin to calm everyone down. *Who is the patient? What happened? Has this happened before?* You're more effective at deciphering the information at the scene—what you see, what you hear, what the patient is telling you. Then you're able to make a more informed decision. You are not rashly treating somebody because of some horrific sign that you see, or some terrible circumstance you've been confronted with. But now by setting the tone, you're able to make a better decision on how to solve the problem and mitigate the situation.

The challenge is this: Set the tone. Instill the confidence in yourself and in others. Take charge of the scene and assume the leadership role that you are obligated to assume. Communicate your needs and implement your plan decisively. And, above all, take care of your patient.

Personal Growth

Personal growth is an extremely important attribute that is critical to being a professional first responder or paramedic. Do not allow personal growth to stop taking place by merely expecting things to happen for you. You have to take a personal interest so you have to invest in yourself. Nobody else can do this for you.

Investing in yourself is important to different aspects of life. You must invest in yourself physically by trying to maintain a healthy exercise routine and a good diet. Exercise is also extremely important to your mental health. If you're not physically capable and feeling physically fit, it can negatively impact you emotionally. Maintaining physical fitness is important for veterans and new medics because stamina allows you to think more clearly and be more engaged because you're not so lethargic and tired.

A sound diet and exercise pay off in dividends for your patients. This doesn't mean that you have to spend hours upon hours at the gym every single day. But it does mean you should have a regular exercise routine—activities to keep yourself physically active. Your diet is also important, so try to eat as healthy as you can. The better your diet, the more energetic you'll feel, and more clearly you will think. This isn't just for your benefit; it is for the benefit of your patients, because you're more capable of thinking clearly when you need to.

Investing in yourself is something that a lot of people talk about but fail to follow through with. You have to take the time to figure out what your goals are and what you want to accomplish and create your own path for success. Nobody else is going to invest in you like you will. You have to take the time to study, to read, and to think through different ideas so that you grow faster.

This is especially true for a paramedic. You have to take the time to go over the different calls that you're going to run and respond to and break them down so that you understand what you're doing and have a better understanding of what happened. Your growth starts with your own understanding of your interpretation of what the calls are that you respond to.

A lot of personal growth will come from self-reflection, which we've discussed earlier in this chapter. Self-reflection will give you better insight into how you think and how you decide to attack certain problems. This can't happen unless you take the time to understand what you did. This way you start to become consistent in your patient care and methodical in how you personally treat patients.

One of the best opportunities for you to grow occurs when you make mistakes. Self-growth happens when you make the mistakes and then grow from them. You're more apt to learn from something that you feel was incorrect, or something that was absolutely incorrect. It's easier to grow from mistakes because errors stand out so glaringly that you recognize your mistake and your need to correct it.

It is important to recognize the mistake, but you have to fix it. You have to identify and respond appropriately to it. You have to take action and take the proper steps in order to understand what went wrong and why, so that those mistakes don't happen again. That doesn't mean that you're not going to make the same mistake again. Instead, you are now actively and intentionally trying to limit the quantity of mistakes, which contributes to developing your method for your decision-making. You have to want to be better; don't ever be satisfied.

Knowledge is important, but it's a small piece of the pie. Knowledge is not what makes people good paramedics. However, knowledge does have its place in relation to personal growth. You have to make sure that you are in a constant state of study and continuing education to make sure that you are always providing the standard of care. Paramedics should want to be in a constant state of learning new ways to accomplish the same objectives. You want to make sure that you're studying all your cardiology and your pharmacology and that you try to become better at these tasks throughout your career. However, we want to stress that knowledge in and of itself is not what makes a good paramedic. It is what you do with that knowledge—through the traits of personal growth—that is more important.

Assessment Skills

Having good assessment skills is an extremely important attribute of a good paramedic. First and foremost you have to understand that yours is a physical job. You're going to have to perform physical exams on your patients. The more that you do this, the easier it becomes and eventually becomes second nature. You have to physically touch your patients in order to properly assess them. This is the only way that you're going to see and feel certain injuries. You don't want to be the paramedic that brings a patient into the hospital with obvious trauma that you didn't find because you didn't do a physical exam.

Lots of times the physical assessment gets overlooked. You have to take the time to develop a method that you consistently use to practice and perform physical exams. Whether it's a head-to-toe assessment on everybody or an assessment based on their chief complaint, you must consistently perform your assessment. This is how you don't miss things. You have to know what you're looking for.

A physical assessment done by a professional paramedic is done with intention. What are you intending to find? Why are you palpating someone's head or neck? Why are you palpating their abdomen? Are you doing it just to go through the motions, or are you doing it with the intention of finding something that is clinically significant? You have to have intention. It's not good enough to just do a physical assessment and run through the motions, because that's how you miss things. If you're not expecting to find something, then sometimes you won't, even if something is present.

That doesn't mean that you're going to find things all the time. In fact, most of the time, you won't. But the more you do it, and the more physical exams you perform, the higher the likelihood is that, when something is wrong, you will pick up on it. You will notice something that's different. You'll notice the crepitus of someone's face because you never felt that before. It will be easier for you to detect the rigid, distended abdomen if you're used to palpating the stomach and making sure that it is soft and nontender. If you make this a routine, it's not a big deal, and when there is something wrong, you're more apt to notice a problem.

An example of the importance of the physical exam is on a seemingly insignificant traffic accident. Many times on minor traffic accidents people have minor complaints or vague complaints. This is where you have to perform your physical exam to make sure that you don't find anything significant. Lots of patients won't exhibit problems because they're just shaken up from being in a traffic accident. This is when you need to do your job, be a professional, and perform a rapid physical assessment looking for major problems. We have found clinically significant injuries on patients with no complaints from traffic accidents so many times we can't even count. It's important for you to not miss these patients because that's what your job is as a professional paramedic or first responder.

You'll still make mistakes. Every honest paramedic working will tell you that they've missed things, and that they will continue to miss something significant, but the idea is to limit the quantity of mistakes. It will also limit the severity of the mistake so that you don't miss big issues. You don't want to miss the patient that has a flail segment. Do not assume they're having trouble breathing because they're anxious from the car accident they just got in. That's not acceptable and that is not being a professional. You should strive for a high standard of patient care.

Your assessment skills go beyond just the physical exam. One of the most critical tasks that we do is gathering the history. Your assessment includes gathering history of the present illness and why emergency services were called. You want to try to figure out and get a clear picture of why someone called 911. Whether or not you believe the call is an emergency is irrelevant, you are there to provide and render care to whoever has called.

The best way to develop good assessment skills and smart methods for gathering history is by doing lots of assessments. Then, after having done the assessments, you have to reflect on why you asked the questions that you asked, what the information was you were trying to obtain, why you thought that it was important, and whether the information was actually important. Then you can start to develop your method. You should try to understand why you decided what to ask, and why you decided what *not* to ask, and why you thought it was important. This is something that only you as the individual paramedic can develop. Everybody has their own unique way of gathering information, and you have to develop an assessment that works for you. Make sure you practice your assessments and questioning with intention.

When you ask a question, listen to what the patient's answer is so that you understand and get the information that you want. We cannot stress this enough. Do not cut your patients off and interrupt them. It is rude and unprofessional. Part of a good assessment is asking questions and then shutting your mouth and listening to what your patient tells you. Just listen to the response. You have to practice active listening. Don't anticipate what the answer will be. Listen to the response instead of thinking about what your next question should be. Your focus should be on the answer to your current question.

Your patient will usually tell you what is going on. You just have to have the patience to listen. Let them tell you what's going on. They will give you the information that you need. Sometimes you have to gently guide your patient, but don't be rude and short with them. How would you feel if it was your grandmother who was sick, and another paramedic cut her off and was short with her when she was explaining to them how she was feeling?

Don't just go through the motions of asking questions because you want to check off the box. Ask questions with the intention of getting information you need to treat your patients. The more you practice your assessment skills, and the more you contemplate why you ask certain questions, the more you're going to get out of it. Your assessment is maybe the most important task that you will do for your patient. Your assessment drives what action needs to take place and what interventions you perform. You have to have good assessments. You have to have sound physical exams and a smart line of questioning. You can practice these techniques on every patient by engaging and really trying to understand what it is you're trying to find out.

Application of Knowledge

The application of knowledge is another attribute that seems trivial and insignificant, even automatic, but really it's not. This is also a skill that has to be developed. Your knowledge of medicine is useless if you don't know how to apply it. It doesn't matter how much you know. It only matters how you apply what you know. Think about this critical concept.

Accumulating knowledge is fruitless if you don't know how to work it into your methodology and your assessment skills. Furthermore, if you accumulate knowledge and are not able to categorize and apply it correctly, your inability actually hinders your patient care because now you are thinking about too many different aspects of what might be going on with the patient instead of just intervening on what you're seeing. One of the biggest problems with paramedics is that they believe knowledge is the key to success. The larger picture eludes them. Knowledge does not make you a good paramedic. It doesn't matter if you can regurgitate information you read in a book. If you cannot apply knowledge correctly in the field, you will not be effective as a paramedic.

Certainly, knowledge is important. There is much to learn didactically in order to succeed, but remember it's useless if you don't know how to apply it. Decisiveness is more important than knowing cardiology at the level of a cardiologist. However, if you can manage and develop both, that is truly incredible. We absolutely encourage you to learn as much as you can, but be humble about it.

A certain amount of knowledge is required in order to be a successful paramedic. You have to know basic pharmacology, basic cardiology, and how these areas interact with each other. You have to know and understand airway management skills. How to do certain procedures. How those procedures are going to affect the patient. But mindless regurgitation of information is really useless. It doesn't matter if you could recite the entire paramedic book or *The Merck Manual* if you don't know how to use the information.

As we have stated, the application of knowledge is a skill that has to be developed. This skill is developed through reflection and understanding of what your process is and how you implement your methodical approach. Why do you do what you do? It also requires the correct interpretation of the information that you gathered from your assessment.

Ability to Act

The ability to act seems like a simple concept, but it is not. This is actually an attribute that has to be developed. This attribute is developed through experience and through a concerted effort to understand what the decisions were that you made. You have to develop the confidence to use your assessment as a tool to identify what is wrong. The ability to act comes from confidence. Your confidence comes from repeating smart decisions and having good outcomes.

The ability to act sounds easy, and for some people it will come easier, but for others it can be difficult. If you struggle with taking action, this is a skill set that you can actively develop. Do not be ashamed if you need to practice. It's okay to have to develop this skill. You can practice by doing little actions on every shift. Just practice giving and conducting certain interventions with intention. For example, if you can't decide when to give Zofran, how on earth will you decide whether to give epinephrine? In other words, if you can't act upon something simple and understand why you're acting upon it, then what confidence do you have that you'll be able to act on something more serious?

You become more confident in your ability to act when it's critical if you practice small actions throughout the day and throughout your career. You can really start to develop your ability to act if you don't downplay the small decisions that you are making. Remember, you are intervening in people's lives, trying to make their situations better. Build upon the intention of the small decisions you make. You will be amazed at how quickly you grow.

In summary, these essential interpersonal skills will serve you well as you develop them. Once again we want to reiterate that we are trying to build an integrated understanding of how to approach patient care. You will be much more capable of expressing your vision for patient care and utilizing your vast medical knowledge. In our experience, developing these skills in yourself and the colleagues you teach will, without a doubt, build your confidence.

Section II

Building a Framework for Success

3

Developing a Process

How do we go about developing a paramedic? There are plenty of different theories about how to do this. And we suppose each individual has their own thoughts and has developed their own process. In this section we will give some clarity and maybe articulate some ideas and thoughts about how to develop a paramedic.

We will talk about many of the processes you may already do, but may not have articulated. This chapter can serve as a basic outline for how to develop a new paramedic. Some of the principles are the same as developing yourself, but now there are some different steps needed. This will be a brief overview of developing another paramedic, and these ideas will be expanded upon later.

One of the first steps in developing a paramedic is having an expectation talk. It is not your job to teach a paramedic medicine. Just to clarify: It is not your job as the preceptor or instructor to teach the student medicine. It is incumbent upon the student to have already learned the information and gained the knowledge needed to be a paramedic. That is why they go through paramedic school. Your job as the preceptor or instructor is to develop your paramedic's thought process and decision-making skills. This is your job—not reteaching them all of the clinical information they've already learned in paramedic school.

Now, if it becomes glaringly obvious that the student has not learned the information needed to become a paramedic, then you have a major problem. In that case, your job is much more difficult if you have to teach them how to become a paramedic, because you're trying to give them the knowledge and understanding and develop their decision-making skills too. If you have students or paramedics that fit these criteria, you have to be up front with them and let them know that their knowledge base is severely lacking. They have to start doing self-study to bring themselves up to speed. This is important because if someone is not willing to invest in themselves and invest their own time to try to gain knowledge and understanding at the basic level—information they should've learned in paramedic school—then you shouldn't be allowing them to treat patients, and you wouldn't allow them to treat your own family.

So you have to start with the expectations talk. The new paramedic must know what your expectations are, and you must know what their expectations are. Remember, this is a two-way street. You can learn just as much from them as they can learn from you. Your expectations should include the student's or new paramedic's current understanding of cardiology, pharmacology, and basic anatomy and physiology. You need to be up front with your students and new paramedics that you are not going to invest your time in teaching them the basics. These students are already way behind the eight ball.

Now this doesn't mean that you shouldn't check their knowledge and make sure that they have gained the proper understanding and have the proper tools while you're teaching them, but the overall goal is to teach them to make decisions, not teach them cardiology. The overall goal is to help them create a thought process and create their own way of thinking through problems and not teach them cardiology and pharmacology. This approach will better serve your student and better serve you. Being a skilled paramedic is not about knowledge; it is about decisiveness. So how do you develop a situation in which you are now evaluating the decision-making by your students or new paramedics?

Let them know that developing their decision-making is the goal. This is accomplished by creating a safe environment for them to have liberty in. Develop a trusting relationship with your student or new paramedic. Your student needs to know that you are not going to demean them and be judgmental about the decisions they make, because this process takes time to develop. The way to show them trust and build trust is allowing the new medic to make decisions and implement treatment plans and follow them through to their conclusions, and to the conclusion of the call. You cannot just tell the student that this is how you will treat them; you have to show them and practice it.

You need to be able to articulate to your student that you are not teaching them to be you; you are trying to teach them to be them; and you are trying to teach them to develop their own decision-making skills. If you harp on items with them that you would do, that they are not doing, then they don't learn decision-making. Instead, they learn how to please you. They don't learn action; they just learn what you would do, and don't develop their own thought processes. They just adapt their understanding of what you want them to do, or what they think you want them to do. This does not help them to grow. In fact, this approach stunts their growth, and then, when they become paramedics on their own, now they have to learn how to work on their own with no instruction and no evaluation of how they're doing or whether they are making good decisions.

If minor misunderstandings or minor errors take place in knowledge of cardiology or pharmacology or whatever area, then you can quickly address those and move forward. The overall goal is not to dwell on someone's medical knowledge. Your time is much better spent investing in their decision-making skills. They should already have the basic knowledge from paramedic school. The student will be able to demonstrate to you their didactic understanding by improving their decisiveness. This is where you as the instructor want to focus.

How do you measure growth? Maybe more importantly, what type of growth do you want to see? The most important type of growth of a paramedic is their confidence and decisiveness. The paramedic must be decisive. Their knowledge will come through continuing education and reading, but you have to really concentrate and work at refining their decision-making and confidence. In order to develop this in students, you have to see where your student is currently. You need to evaluate how confident they are now. You can do this by seeing how they interact with your patients: Are they calm or are they erratic in their decision-making and nervous? Allow the student time to understand why they made the choices that they made and how those choices impacted the patient. Allow your students the freedom to tell you why they made the choices they did. Concentrate your efforts on helping students understand the decisions made, and why they were made, and as a paramedic they will grow much faster and become much more decisive.

An efficient way to evaluate growth is through consistency. Are they building upon their previous experiences and their understanding of the previous decisions made? Growth is demonstrated also by having the ability to act quicker and more decisively. This is evidence that confidence is growing. Give the students room to fail without sacrificing patient care, and they will learn much quicker. You can evaluate growth also with whether someone is repeating mistakes. Are the students actually developing new habits, or do they continue to make bad decisions or remain unsure of themselves?

One of the culminating factors of growth comes in the form of accountability that you convey to your students. Do you take responsibility for the decisions that you make and are you open about it? If you are willing to take responsibility for decisions, you should know why you made those choices in the first place, and what you saw that made you choose what course of action to implement.

Individual Process

How do you as the individual paramedic become better? How do you become more successful? Many of you who are reading this book are extremely successful and confident paramedics; however, we think that you can still benefit if you have an articulated idea of how to continue to grow. We think that it can benefit everyone to have a tangible, realistic process for continued development. For those of you who are new to prehospital medicine or firefighting or new to being a paramedic, this process can help you to grow quicker and have fewer pitfalls along the way.

We want to make sure that we are giving you a process that is easy to implement and is also reproducible. What we will set forth here is a four-step process to try to develop yourself as a new paramedic or improve your development if you are a seasoned paramedic. This is a process that we use continually and try to instill in the individuals we instruct, whether directly or indirectly.

Be honest with yourself. Number one. You guessed it, you must be honest with yourself. This goes hand-in-hand with all of the personal attributes that we have talked about—humility and integrity being at the forefront. You must be humble enough to understand that you don't know everything, and that's perfectly okay.

What you need to do now is be honest with yourself and figure out what you are deficient in and what actions you can take to improve that area. We have set forth three primary principles to utilize in order to be successful. Just as a quick reminder those three principles are didactic understanding, interpersonal skills and personal attributes, and decision-making.

One of the intriguing aspects about being in emergency situations is that you cannot maintain perfection all of the time. There's always room for improvement, and there's always room for growth. Even the most seasoned and competent paramedic or first responder cannot maintain these three principles perfectly all the time. There's always more to learn. So, first, be honest with yourself and figure out what your biggest weaknesses are. What do you believe that you are deficient in?

[Sam's story] I can tell you that my biggest deficiency is by far pharmacology. I struggle with pharmacology. For whatever reason it is difficult for me to retain all of the different types of medications that people are on, and all of the different side effects and interactions people can have with those medications. Pharmacology is difficult for me. I find myself constantly looking up medications that most of you probably remember easily. At the end of many calls, I will come back to the station and look up medications. I find I also look up medications to figure out what the potential side effects are for some of the patients that we go on. This deficiency would lie in the principle of didactic understanding. I routinely go through my medical guidelines to make sure I have the correct understanding and knowledge of pharmacology.

So what are you deficient in? Be honest with yourself, whether it is didactic understanding or interpersonal skills or a personal attribute that you believe you need to improve upon. After identifying what you are deficient in, you must take actions to improve it. Whether it's study and continuing education for didactic understanding. Or communication skills and interpersonal skills that you can try to develop with your teammates. Or a personal attribute that you want to develop further, that you want to methodically implement and make sure is in the forefront of your thoughts when you go out the door. There's always room for improvement, and this is the first step to developing your individual process. Never settle for how good you are now—always strive to be better.

Set goals and expectations. The second step in developing your process is to set goals and expectations for yourself. This is much like setting goals and expectations for your students or for a new paramedic that you are training if you happen to be a preceptor. Many of the principles remain the same, but now you must implement them for yourself.

A quick word on the difference between a goal and an expectation. An expectation is something that you as the provider want to maintain. It should not fluctuate that much. An example of this would be that it is expected that you do not swear or curse at your patients. A goal is something that you are intentionally working toward accomplishing. An example of this would be trying to establish five differential diagnoses on every patient you go on for the day.

The world of prehospital medicine is so large that we can always set goals and expectations for ourselves. Within the three principles that we've laid out, there are virtually limitless goals and expectations to set forth. These don't necessarily need to be in areas that you are deficient in. But whatever you are deficient in, you must maintain and make goals and expectations to improve. Don't just think about it, write it down. Write it down so that your goals are at the forefront of your thoughts and your actions. When you write down your goals and expectations, you automatically become more accountable to yourself. You can have multiple goals going at one time, so don't think that you have to focus only on one thing at a time.

Create and execute a plan. The third step in developing your process is to create and execute a plan for how you are going to meet your goals and your expectations. You have to conscientiously think about what you want to accomplish. You must intentionally work on the areas that you are deficient in until you meet your goal.

If you have a daily goal, every single time you go on a call, you want to think about what that goal is and try to meet it. You want to write down your goals so that you are better able to execute your plan to meet the goal. In our experience if you write your goals down, they become much more realistic, and it's easier to execute a plan to accomplish the goal. You want to write down the steps needed in order to accomplish your goal. Even writing a simple outline is invaluable because it forces you to start executing.

Reevaluate. The fourth step in developing a process for yourself is to reevaluate. You must reevaluate what you are trying to accomplish. You want to see whether or not your plan is working. You might have a good plan, but you might have bad execution, so now you need to adjust. You might have good execution, but the plan might not be very good. You want to reevaluate what you are intentionally trying to improve upon.

During your self-evaluation, do you find that you are now feeling more comfortable with your deficiencies? Have you met your goal and your expectation of what you wanted to improve? If so, then that is fantastic. Now you must reevaluate something new that you might be deficient in. And take on a new challenge in order to improve that area of your profession.

These four steps are extremely simple and reproducible. These are easy enough for you to do by yourself, but it is much more valuable if you include your teammates. Remember, be honest with yourself and try to improve upon something that you are deficient in. Once you improve on that area, then find something new to develop in yourself. These four steps are a useful process by which you can bring about continued development in prehospital medicine. These steps are easy to understand intellectually, but for drastic growth and understanding to take place, you must implement them with intention. Intend to be better, intend to improve. When you do that, you will grow.

We'll take a look at an example of these four steps in action.

1. Be honest with yourself: You look at your ability to interpret 12-lead EKGs honestly and believe that you need to improve upon it.

2. Set goals and expectations: After recognizing this deficiency, you set the goal of studying 12 leads for fifteen minutes a day for one month. After doing so, it is expected that you no longer misinterpret 12 leads or miss a STEMI.

3. Create and execute a plan: Your plan now is to find an EKG book that you can study. You then compare all of your patient 12 leads and make sure you are interpreting them appropriately. You also make a plan to meet with your medical division to reach out for additional material that will help you learn to interpret 12-lead EKGs. You also go to the medical division and ask for a randomized 12-lead EKG test to get a baseline.

4. Reevaluate: After one month of study, you go back to the medical division and ask for another randomized 12-lead EKG test to see if you have improved. After reevaluating you find that you didn't execute by reading the fifteen minutes a day that you planned. So you did not improve and your goal was not met. Now you have to start over and come up with a plan that you will actually execute and that is realistic for you so that you can improve.

Methodical Approach

A methodical approach is similar to consistency. However, a methodical approach is more of a narrow or focused understanding of how to approach the specific patient. Consistency is more of a global understanding of how to approach each event or call. A methodical approach allows you to be more focused with your specific assessment.

Based on the patient's chief complaint, you can begin to understand what interventions you need to accomplish. So this is much more narrow and focused than a global understanding of consistency. However your methodical approach needs to be consistent. You need to have a basic understanding of the patient's chief complaint in order to methodically approach how you're going to treat them.

An example of the differences that are being discussed is this: Are you methodical in your assessment of the patient with shortness of breath? Do you listen to lung sounds? Do you get SPO2? These interventions are some of the methods that you use to get information on a patient with difficulty breathing. But are you consistent in assessing all of your difficulty-breathing patients with the same method? How is it that you always know when to give Albuterol? Because you are consistent in the methodical assessment of your difficulty-breathing patient.

As you can see, developing a methodical approach on how you interact with each patient is important. Another example is how you do a trauma assessment. We were all taught in our EMT basic school to develop a methodical approach on how you interact with each patient. A common methodical trauma assessment is a head-to-toe approach. We were all taught we start with the head, move down to the chest and abdomen, look at the pelvis, look at the extremities, and then look at the posterior. This is the method by which to assess the trauma patient. Without implementing a methodical approach on every trauma patient, we then begin to miss things.

The point here is not for everybody to have the same method. The point is that everybody is different, and we all treat patients differently. We all have different experiences and ways of interpreting information. The key is for each individual to develop their own method. And, as we've talked about before, the way to develop this method is through general and self-reflection. Whatever method you create, you want to implement it *consistently*.

When you as the new paramedic or the seasoned paramedic develop a methodical approach to patient care, you then understand why you perform and assess patients the way you do. You'll understand better why you gave aspirin to one chest pain patient and withheld aspirin from a different chest pain patient. The key is that if you implement a methodical approach to patient care, the patients that need aspirin will be identified and you will give it. You want to take the time to develop this technique and then implement it consistently.

If you're methodical, you can train yourself to interpret information more quickly and more accurately. Being methodical as a paramedic goes far beyond patient care. In this day and age you have to be methodical about how you approach houses, how you approach traffic accidents, and how you approach unseen variables. It is critical to approach these situations for your own safety and for the safety of your team. Are you methodical about how you look for weapons? In a house? Or on your patient? Or which patients you search? Are you methodical about safety on a traffic accident? What methods do you use to consistently mitigate the risks that paramedics see on a daily basis?

Creating these methods for you as an individual will make you better at every aspect of the job. Having a methodical approach allows you to identify abnormalities. As a paramedic you are always dealing with what might be abnormal to the general public, but it becomes normal for you. Being methodical allows you to identify when something is not right—on a medical or a traffic accident or any scene you go on. Even if you can't put your finger on it, you know something is not right. That sixth sense is honed by being methodical about your approach.

This is an ever-changing attribute. You have to refine this skill on a regular basis. Such refinement comes by integrating all these attributes that we are currently exploring. There are plenty of reasons for this refinement. EMS is a constantly changing environment, whether it is from social issues, political issues, or always ever-changing medical guidelines and protocols. You will be a better paramedic if you try to develop and identify your methodical approach.

Most of you do these practices subconsciously already, but have you taken the time to think about it? Most importantly, do you stress this approach with new paramedics and try to give them the proper feedback so that they can create their own methods? Each of us is different, so making a new paramedic or a student use your methods is much less beneficial for them and for you. Let us not forget that you can learn just as much from a new paramedic or student as they can from a seasoned veteran.

When training a new paramedic, it is vitally important to give them the latitude to develop their own style and methods. The veteran paramedic will also learn new ways to do things. The trainer or preceptor must be confident in their own skills and understanding to be able to create a fruitful learning environment for a student to develop their own methods.

Consistency

Consistency is a global personal character attribute that describes how you approach a problem, lifestyle, or situation. Being consistent with something could be as easy as consistently reading a book, consistently studying 12-lead EKGs, consistently checking your gear out, consistently checking your medications. Consistency is the *what*; whereas, methodology is the *how*. You can consistently wake up early in the morning, but the method you use is an alarm clock. Consistency is an attribute, and methodology is how that attribute is achieved or displayed.

Consistency is extremely important for the development of a paramedic. Consistency goes hand-in-hand with developing a methodical approach for patient assessment. To be consistent, you have to be able to approach different patients and different situations similarly. You want to develop consistency because then you're not floundering around on all the different calls you go on. You begin to build confidence in what you're doing because you're consistent.

Your consistency starts to develop with the more experience you gain and the reflection that you have on the calls that you go on. Consistency is important because you're able to duplicate how you interact with patients, how you interact with the public, and how you interact with different situations. If you never develop consistency, then every call you run will be as if it's the first time you've ever seen something. If you develop consistency, then every time you intubate someone, you will know what to expect, and then if a problem comes up, you are better able to overcome it. Consistency allows you to build upon every single call, especially calls that are similar in nature.

Another aspect of consistency is developing trust, especially within your team. If you are a preceptor, consistency also develops trust with your student or preceptee. Your team has a better understanding of what to expect from you as the paramedic. If you approach situations consistently, your teammates will be better able to anticipate and address what your needs are and what your needs will be. It will also develop their own skills and their own understanding of what is going on with the patient. This overall development is essential for a better patient care environment.

Consistency allows teamwork to prevail because your team will be able to anticipate all your needs. And when you approach calls consistently, your teammates are not constantly looking for supervision or guidance from you. Consistency creates an environment that allows your team to work independently from you because they know what to expect from you and what you require of them. If you're inconsistent in your approach, they will be in a constant state of needing your guidance, which hinders your team's ability to function.

When consistency is used in an integrated practice along with humility, you as a practitioner will become extremely successful. Why? Simply. You will miss things, you will make mistakes, you will come up short. This is where your teammates come in, because your humble and consistent approach in the past has set the standard of care. When you inevitably deviate from that standard, for whatever reason, your teammates will more easily be able to recognize it and address the deviation. And since you display humility, you will react accordingly. What is the result? Better paramedicine, better teamwork, and certainly better patient care.

If you approach situations with a consistent manner, you're also less likely to miss critical details. If you constantly run calls where you are feeling as if you are starting over and over and you're never gaining any understanding, you have to develop a consistent manner to approach those calls. If you're inconsistent in the way that you approach calls, it's going to affect so many other aspects of your patient care because you'll become less confident, and then your lack of confidence affects your ability to act. To develop a paramedic properly, you have to have an integrated understanding of how all these moving parts work.

In summary, use this four-step process to help you improve any skill that you feel is deficient in your practice. Whether it is medical knowledge or communication skills for delegation and leadership, we encourage you to use this process to develop yourself. Your practice should be founded in the methodical approach and then implement those methods consistently. Understand that you can have different methods for how you treat different types of patients (such as a respiratory patient versus a trauma patient).

4

Building Confidence

Whether you are training somebody else or you need to build confidence in your own practice, it's extremely important to develop confidence in your work. One of the best ways to build confidence in yourself and in the people you are training is to allow them to make decisions freely. You have to create an environment in which your students have the liberty to practice and make decisions that they will make when you're not around. By allowing them to make the decisions, you are building their confidence in what they're doing, in how their thought process is interpreting each patient, and how their thought process is creating their personal treatment plan for each patient that they encounter.

If you're having trouble with confidence personally, one of the best exercises you can do is make small decisions and then understand why you made those small decisions in each patient. Not every decision you make is going to be groundbreaking or life altering or even intervening on critical patients, but if you concentrate and understand why you make little decisions, it will build your confidence so that you can make big decisions. This practice goes hand-in-hand with analyzing the decisions that you do make, whether they're big or small—understand what information you gathered in order to make the decision that you made. This takes a little bit of effort and a little more work, but you will reap the benefit of understanding why you do what you do, and why you take the actions that you do. These seemingly little decisions that you make will be easier and easier to build upon if you understand.

A simple example would be responding to a lift assist where instead of just picking the patient up off the floor, you saw something that made you want to take a blood pressure and a set of vitals, and then because of those abnormal readings, you then made the patient a patient instead of just a lift assist. This may seem like a small endeavor, but if you break it down and try to figure out why you did what you did, and what you saw that made you make the decision to check further instead of doing a simple lift assist, and what made you decide to take a set of vital signs, it will help you in your overall understanding of how you make decisions and how your mind works. Such practices will give you a better understanding of how you are interpreting information. This is a small example, but if you can do small ones like this, you will make it easier to make big decisions.

Building confidence is also really incumbent upon the teacher. In this sense we mean that as the teacher or instructor you have to create a safe learning environment (discussed further in chapter 8). Building a safe learning environment really gives your students the liberty they need in order to make decisions, and this is one of the key factors in building their confidence, which is also a key factor for you to build your own confidence.

Building confidence in yourself and building confidence in the people you train has one important aspect that must always be integrated in your teaching, and that is feedback. Providing feedback to your students is a critical step that they need to build confidence. There are really two types of feedback when you break it down: negative feedback and positive feedback. This idea is paramount to your students' growth. However, this can also be integrated into your own growth because providing feedback to your students is a critical step that they need in order to build confidence.

[Chris's story] As an example, I routinely ask the physicians that I hand patients off to if there was anything I could have done better, if there was anything that I missed, or if there's anything else that they would like me to do next time. I also routinely ask other paramedics that I work with what their thoughts are on different calls. I engage with other paramedics I work with to try to give them feedback when they ask me questions. Feedback is a two-way street, and it's important to provide constructive feedback. Sure, it's easy to focus on negative feedback because you will see things that maybe you don't like that your student is doing, or your student is doing something differently than you would do it, so it's easy to provide negative feedback.

If your students have glaring problems, then make sure you're addressing them appropriately and providing them feedback on what they might be doing wrong. However, it's equally as important, if not more important, to provide them with positive reinforcement. You have to let them know about the practices they are doing well. People are encouraged when other people encourage them and when other people and teachers specifically reinforce what they are doing right. Providing both positive and negative feedback is critical to building confidence. This has to be an ongoing process. Even as you become a seasoned paramedic, you have to be constantly looking for (and giving) feedback.

One of the best ways that you can build confidence and that confidence can be demonstrated is by allowing your students to build upon the feedback that you're giving them. You have to subtly guide your students with feedback. After providing feedback to your students, make sure that you are allowing them the liberty to exercise and demonstrate their confidence and growth by giving you examples of it. When students demonstrate examples of growth, through actions, it reassures you as the instructor that your feedback is being digested.

Another way to really develop confidence in yourself and the students that you will encounter is to provide reasonable solutions to struggles and difficulties. It builds confidence in your students to see that there are reasonable and rational solutions to the situations that they face. This builds confidence by letting them know that it is possible to not feel as if they are always drowning. The way to build this confidence is to help provide those solutions for people who are struggling with how to make decisions and are struggling with which treatment plans to implement.

If you are the type of paramedic for whom these things come easy, then take pride in the fact that people come to you to help instruct what they should be doing. Don't talk down or demean people when they ask you questions about what you think they should be doing or how you think they should handle a situation. Nobody reacts well if you're condescending. You should act professional and take pride and be humbled by the opportunity to benefit one of your coworkers.

Remember, this goes back to what we have talked about before: You're not better than anybody else. You do not have more intrinsic value than anybody else, so just help them out. Help them build their confidence by understanding that there are reasonable and rational solutions to the situations that they come across. If you do this, and you do it in a gentle way, and you are not boastful, you'll develop great confidence in your coworkers—and you will also develop confidence in yourself.

Invest in yourself to work through your own understanding of why, how, and what you do on each call. Allow your students time to reflect upon their own understanding. Do not give your students answers but allow them to work through the process of finding the answer for themselves. Not everything in paramedicine has a straightforward answer. After time and experience, clarity forms and things become clear. What happens is that your confidence gives you good discernment, and then you realize there really is no gray area. Your students will be much better off if you allow them the ability to find the answers on their own with your subtle, gentle guidance. Indecision is not an option. Making a decision is the most important attribute of a successful paramedic.

Building confidence is really a combination of a couple of different attributes. One is hard work. A good work ethic builds confidence that you are prepared to meet the challenges that you will face. A good work ethic with the factors that you can control such as your equipment, your uniform, and your sleep will give you confidence that you are going to be able to face whatever gets thrown your way. Most importantly, a good work ethic gives you the confidence that you are not taking shortcuts.

Dedication to continuing education and continual investment in yourself will build confidence in your abilities. You have to dedicate and discipline yourself to become better, so never be satisfied with the paramedic that you are now. Build good habits and practice those habits. When you practice good habits, that habitual event becomes subconscious. Sometimes you will have to conscientiously, willfully implement better habits. Some good habits are more difficult to form than others.

In our experience the habits that are difficult to form are usually the ones that are more important. When you start your shift, if you willfully practice the habits that you want, they will become easier. One of the best side effects is that it becomes contagious, not only for you but for your crew or your partner. Discipline yourself to practice good habits, and they will absolutely build your confidence.

Ownership is a difficult attribute to attain because we are prone to excuses. Ownership is so crucial to confidence. Ownership provides the understanding that, whatever happens, you will take responsibility. The by-product is that it reduces or eliminates excuses for actions you take, which will greatly build your confidence.

If you conduct yourself as a professional, you will build confidence. You must see yourself as a professional. Being professional develops helpful habits and sound routines. It forces you to take events seriously and to engage with each call that you respond to. Professionalism will build your confidence because, when the alarm goes off, you know it's game time.

5

There Is No Gray

Everything you encounter in EMS as a paramedic is black and white. There is no gray, only indecision. Indecision causes you to think that unfolding events are muddled or convoluted. Indecision causes you to think there are more difficult choices than there really are. Looking at situations and believing that things are gray is really just an expression of indecision. You just lack the decisiveness to act.

Your interpretation of what is a perceived gray situation is really an inability to interpret information properly and then make an informed decision. What it really boils down to is a lack of accountability. You don't want to make a decision that might be wrong, so you put off making a decision and chalk it up to a gray situation. You become paralyzed with fear of consequences. Your fear manifests with indecision. Your indecision compromises patient care. Again, there is no gray, only indecision.

Either you care for your patients' best interests or not. This indecision clearly demonstrates a lack of working knowledge of the job. Do you understand your scope of practice? Your decision-making process should not include a foundation of fear; it should be founded upon confidence. If you lack confidence, you must ask yourself if you are a person who embodies these important principles as set forth in this book. Your confidence is built upon work. Work on your work ethic. Your integrity. Your self-reflection and growth. Work on these and you will become more decisive. You will see there is no gray, only indecision.

What kind of provider are you? One who lacks the willingness to make a decision for your patients' best interests? Or one who is always concerned with your own self-serving ambitions or needs? Here, too, there is no gray. Your indecision is demonstrative of where your priorities lie. Let's be clear. If you do not make someone a patient who should be, your tell is up. Your indecision and self-serving interests are on display. This is a reflection of lack of professionalism.

Your lack of decisiveness creates more problems for you, and the lack of decisiveness is contagious. When you are indecisive, it silently gives other providers on scene the liberty to make excuses for their own indecision. This problem then perpetuates itself, and patient care in the entire system declines.

When you become enamored with the idea that things are gray and muddled, and it's difficult to navigate what to do on specific calls, what you're really concerned with is the judgment of your peers. You're concerned with what your peers will say about what you chose to do in a given situation. You're concerned with what your medical director might say, or that you might get in trouble. Your concern is with whether or not your medical division is going to question what you've done. Here's a newsflash: They should question what you're doing because that's how you grow.

If you're not challenging yourself, you're not in a state of self-growth. Being a paramedic is a constant state of growth in a constant state of change. You must learn to embrace change and welcome change. Everything you do in your career is going to change, from the medicine to the way we treat people.

If you are acting decisively within your guidelines and within your protocols, it's going to make work much easier for you. You have to be able to interpret the information that you are given appropriately and then decide what to do. Much of your indecisiveness is due to a lack of proper understanding of what your job is. Your job is not necessarily to specifically diagnose people with an ailment. You have to understand that your job is to find life threats and then treat them accordingly. You are working in emergency situations.

One of the most common, if not the most common, problems that we come across is people's lack of understanding when it comes to refusals. The reason people are indecisive about refusals is because they have failed to understand what constitutes a proper refusal. Most paramedic schools do not go into detail about what this means. It's actually very black and white and not gray. You just haven't taken the time to articulate it, to construct a methodical approach with how you refuse patients.

It's simple to take the easy way out and say that someone is not a patient when they really are. Depending on what your protocols state or your guidelines require of you, you may or may not have to do refusals on anybody who has a complaint. What it really boils down to is having to decide who can refuse and who cannot refuse. Don't make this gray.

In order to approach this dilemma methodically, you have to start with a mental status exam. Does somebody have the mental capacity and mental faculties in order to refuse? This is not a difficult question and should not be hard to understand.

Just because someone can tell you who the president is or what city they live in does not necessarily mean that they can refuse treatment. This is one of the biggest hang-ups that new paramedics and even seasoned paramedics come across.

Many paramedics believe that these situations are gray because they don't know what to do with patients who are not acting appropriately but can answer all your questions. They don't understand why somebody can be taken to the hospital if they can answer all your questions. They don't understand that it's really your obligation to make sure that these people are getting the appropriate care. It doesn't matter if someone can tell you who the president is, that does not mean that they automatically can refuse. There's more to it than that.

The patient has to be calm, they have to be cooperative, and they have to be able to demonstrate an understanding of the situation that they are in and be able to understand what the reasonable risks of refusing are. Assessing for these traits is easy to do if you don't make it gray with indecision. But people muddy it up and make it gray because they lack the ability to act. And honestly what it really boils down to is they don't want to do the work. They have fear. They fear the idea of someone telling them they will be sued for kidnapping.

Hold on tight for a second, we are going to make a statement here that you need to understand. WE DO NOT KIDNAP PEOPLE. WE TAKE THEM TO THE HOSPITAL. We are not taking people to Mexico and then asking for ransom. Your fear of this is an excuse for inaction. If you want to be a professional, you must understand that you are obligated to intervene for people. This is especially true for patients that lack decision-making capability and are unable to care for themselves. This is the definition of implied consent. It is implied that they want you to take care of them. To drive this point home, we will make another statement. The paramedic who fails to act in these situations lacks conviction. They lack the conviction that they are now obligated to intervene for those who cannot intervene for themselves.

That's what it really boils down to. So are you going to do your job and fulfill what is required of you or not? Confidence plays a key role in whether or not you perceive situations as black and white or gray. You have to be confident in the decisions that you're making and that you're making the best decision for all of your patients that you interact with.

Either someone has a complaint or they don't. Black and white, not gray. Either someone is a patient or they are not. Either they can refuse treatment and transport or they can't. This is not difficult to understand. If they meet refusal requirements for your jurisdiction, then they can refuse. Don't try to dance around the system that is in place for where you work. Instead, embrace the system and work within it.

If you try to get out of working and try to get out of doing the paperwork, it just makes life more difficult for you. It causes you to be indecisive. All this stems from an improper attitude toward the work that you're supposed to be doing. If someone meets the criteria, then do the paperwork. If you are required by your medical directors to do paperwork, then do the paperwork. The real question is whether you are going to be a professional. How are you going to conduct yourself? If you implement this mentality, you'll start to see that the calls you go on are not gray—they're extremely black and white.

The patient who is tripping out on meth and has an erratic thought process is going to the hospital. You can see this as you pull on scene. This isn't difficult to understand, but if you lack the decisiveness and you lack the proper mentality of work, you chalk it up to a gray situation. Who can make sense of these things? Just do your best. These ideas are infectious about how you should operate. Don't tell yourself, *I think they'll be okay.*

You have to flush this idea of gray from your system, and you have to flush this mentality from your work ethic. If you can properly apply these principles to the way you approach patients, when you do come across a situation that is convoluted, it will make it easier for you to decide what to do, because you can rely on the decision-making process that you have developed. You understand basic principles like chief complaint, patient refusal, mental status, and the ability to refuse, and you are able to rely on your good work ethic knowing that you are not making decisions based on what the workload is. This will inevitably make you a better paramedic. Practicing this skill will make you more reliable and consistent. This is the method that you use to consistently evaluate situations, and as you do it, situations will become clearer.

One of the basic tenets that we try to practice in approaching every call is this: If the thought of the paperwork enters your mind or the concern about paperwork goes through your mind because you know your action is going to cause you to do more, you must force yourself to do it. If you don't force yourself to do the work, you are subconsciously talking yourself out of doing something you know you should be doing. Whether that is a refusal, whether it is making somebody a patient, and whether that is advising somebody to be transported to the hospital, you're doing something against what you know you should be doing if you are concerned with the paperwork involved.

Forcing yourself to commit to doing this work can be difficult, but if you conscientiously try to, it becomes easier. If this concern is at the forefront and you habitually practice overcoming it, your thought becomes habit and then it becomes routine for you and then it's not a big deal. Then that's just how you operate. It also provides your team with a consistent way to measure what's going to take place on any given call. Because you're consistent with them, as we have said in many other ways, they are more easily able to help you.

Another basic tenant that we practice routinely is this: If a person has a complaint, they are a patient. If they are a patient, they either get transported or they get refused. If they get refused, they have to meet the refusal criteria—that is, whatever your medical directors have stipulated in respect to refusals. If someone meets these criteria, it's easy to refuse them. The big issue is to stop trying to get out of work. The perceived gray situations or lack of decisiveness will cause you more problems, and in critical situations can produce hesitation. The lack of decisiveness comes from trying to talk yourself out of doing something you know you should be doing.

Gray situations are really not gray. Develop a process that can be repeated to make sound decisions in convoluted situations. Understand the intent of your medical division, the intent of your medical directors, and what your capabilities are as far as discernment within any given situation. If you understand the intent of these people, you will be able to develop a process that is repeatable and reliable. You have to be able to reproduce basic concepts so that situations don't seem gray.

In the end, discerning the proper disposition of your patients and having the proper interpretation of each call will cause you to sleep better at night. You won't be concerned about whether or not you made the right decision because you were able to decide with confidence. You are in a position where you have to decide what to do with people, and then after deciding, you have to own it.

If you demonstrate understanding of the intent of your medical division, and your medical directors, you become much more reliable and more trustworthy to them. They understand and will be able to see that you're demonstrating the ability to make the right decisions and that you are exercising discernment. This is a key concept. You must understand what the intent is of your physician advisors and your medical division, if applicable. If you do not fully understand what they want from you in specific situations, it is incumbent upon you to ask them. Take ownership and be the professional and ask them for clarity. Have your physician advisors and medical divisions communicated to you what their intent is? If not, you must ask so you can work freely within the guidelines that they set forth.

When it comes to medical and trauma patients, quickly identify what the problems are and then act. If you think that the situation is gray because you're unable to determine whether someone is a cardiac patient or a respiratory patient, choose. You need to choose something to treat. A lack of intervention and a lack of acting and the inability to act is a decision. On sick medical and sick trauma patients, you need to intervene. Don't make these situations gray—they're black and white. Take this approach, and you'll develop better skills, quicker.

6

Principles of Decision-Making

Making decisions comes easy for some people, but for others it is difficult. Lots of factors affect how someone comes to make a decision. Consider this question: What makes a good decision? In this chapter we will develop a process for you to make a decision.

Experience

One of the biggest factors that's going to affect how you make your decisions is your experience. Your decisions will be based largely on what you have seen before. Presumably you have gone through a school in which you had to be mentored by a paramedic or multiple paramedics who tried to develop your skill set. Many of you reading this book have been EMT basics for many years, and some of you went straight to paramedic. Those of you who were an EMT basic prior to going to paramedic school can use your experience as EMT basics to draw on. A lack of experience, however, does not mean that you will make bad decisions. Likewise, experience in and of itself does not automatically mean that you're always going to make good decisions. Experience also does not necessarily mean that you have developed a process to make decisions. Experience really benefits those who learn from their experiences and try to develop and articulate the system for success.

Experience can help you make decisions, because when you come across a situation that you've not seen before, you're able to try to paint a picture based on something you have seen. You can decide what to do based on what you've seen before. Or if you've not directly had experience that you can draw from, experiences that other people have had, if they share them with you, can inform you of how they dealt with a certain situation. Again, reflect on new experiences; this will cause self-growth and develop your own personal decision-making.

Experiences of others can be greatly beneficial to you if you allow them to filter through your understanding. We've talked in great detail of ego and humility, and this is one of those cases in which you allow somebody else's experiences to help you form an idea of how you will decide what to do in those situations that you've not seen but others have. Not all of us will see every single situation as a paramedic. For example, not everyone will perform RSI (rapid sequence intubation) or see status seizures. Not everyone will work on an ambulance or work in the hospital. There are far too many situations and variables that happen for you to gain experience on every type of call. This is why it's important to gain experience through others who have had encounters that you might not have had, but potentially could have. You will be better equipped to deal with those circumstances when they arise if you learn from others' experiences.

Experience, however, can be a double-edged sword. Experience has a tendency to allow you to become indifferent toward what you're seeing. This again comes down to ownership and professionalism. You have to allow these two ideas to permeate your understanding of how to be a paramedic. This way your vast amount of experience does not cause you to become jaded; it does not become useless because you are now indifferent toward your patient. These two components also allow for others to grow through you, and you are better equipped to mentor other responders.

Experience can, of course, have a negative outcome if you become overconfident in what your capabilities are. Becoming overconfident with what you can do can cause people serious harm. It is a bad decision to delay definitive care for a patient because you are acting outside of your capabilities. Or are so confident in your abilities that you delay the definitive care that a patient really needs.

A simple example of overconfidence is delaying care to a STEMI (ST Elevation Myocardial Infarction) alert and taking your time getting to the hospital because you are confident that, if something happens, you will be able to handle it. Being a paramedic is not about what you can or cannot handle. It is about providing care to a patient while you are getting them to definitive care quickly. Delaying care happens when somebody becomes overconfident because they do not allow their experiences to be properly managed and utilized, and they believe that because they've seen and done so many of these runs that they're able to handle all sorts of problems without the need for definitive care.

As a paramedic, you are not going to be able to fix certain situations in the field. Despite what your experience level is, we don't have the capabilities, training, and knowledge to act as definitive care. If you integrate your understanding of experience, capabilities, knowledge, and training, you can make better decisions. Bad decisions are made when people work outside of their capability, outside of their scope of practice, and allow their experience to dictate to them what they think should happen despite what their training says.

Bad decisions also come from experience by telling you that something is not as serious as it looks just because last time, when you saw a similar scenario, it was no big deal. You always have to have a healthy balance of experience and index of suspicion. Just because you have seen something a hundred times does not mean that the 101st time it's not going to go bad on you. You don't have to be overly aggressive, but you should remain professional and ready for any negative outcomes that may come your way.

Another key element of experience is not merely witnessing or seeing a call run, but you have to become involved in every call that you go on. There is an important distinction here that we need to make. Consider the big difference between responding to a call and running a call. If you are merely responding and not engaging in the decision-making process, you will not develop nearly as fast, if at all. Watching someone else make decisions does not by default give you the same ability or understanding.

Your experience will grow greatly and quicker if you involve yourself in the calls that you're responding to. You can't sit on the sideline as a secondary or tertiary responder and think that everyone is gaining the same experience from the call that's in front of you. That's like saying you can gain experience in football because you watched a football game. Although you may develop a somewhat deeper understanding of football by watching the game take place, you don't deceive yourself into thinking you have the same understanding or experience in the game as the actual players or coaches. The game unfolds as it does, but the experiences of those participating in the event—whether it's by playing, coaching, or observing—are completely different.

You must understand this. You have to become involved, so don't sit and simply observe. In the football game you may sit back and tell yourself, "I would have run a different play or thrown to a different receiver." But you don't truly think your understanding of what is taking place within the game is actually greater than the coach or player. It's much easier to make decisions and critiques when you're not the one actually making the true decision or responsible for calling the play.

Such active decision-making can be difficult sometimes for those who work in systems that have multiple agencies that respond to the same patient. This is where your ego has to be put in check. It will benefit you, the other agencies, and the patient to work together as a team. In most situations the paramedic who makes first contact with the patient should maintain patient care and be the lead paramedic. This doesn't mean that the lead paramedic makes all the decisions or makes all the decisions by themselves, but they should be the one in the lead so that the patient understands who they're dealing with, which causes less confusion for the patient. You can hand the patient off to a transporting agency, or you can help the transporting agency with whatever they need because they beat you first on scene. You have to work together as a team. This will help everyone involved develop experience making decisions.

Decisions and experience cannot be gained by watching someone else. You have to be involved in making decisions or helping make the decision for what is going to happen with the patient. If you put yourself in positions where you are now gaining experience, you need to break down the calls that you're running and try to understand what you decided to do and why (the attribute of self-reflection we discussed earlier). When you do so, you'll understand what you're trying to accomplish better and you'll understand your own personal process for making decisions (again, the attribute of self-growth).

Your assessment skills and your interventions and treatment plans will build through your experience and then improve your ability as a paramedic. The experience you have, if properly used, will directly affect your confidence, and your confidence will directly affect your ability to make the right decisions in bad situations. If you are confident that you have made good decisions in the past based on your experiences, you could be confident that what you're doing now in a given situation is a good decision because you have taken the time to develop your process. Experience is important but not the only factor.

Information

Another factor that drives decision-making is information. Do you have enough information to make a decision? Do you have too little information? Do you have too much information in that it causes you to not be able to act? You have to ensure that you have enough information to actually start developing your treatment plan.

Your treatment plan is going to be what you are deciding to do for your patient. Sometimes this can happen quickly, and sometimes it takes a lot of questioning to try to understand and get the information needed in order to make a decision on what type of treatment the patient might need. Before moving forward, you need to have at least some information to be able to decide how to move forward. If you have too little information, you might treat the patient in a way that is harmful.

You also have to have information about the patient and about their specific condition so that you can treat them appropriately—such as their allergies so you don't give them a medication that they're allergic to. Before you decide what to do, you have to have some information and not just act arbitrarily without any information.

Now this doesn't mean that everybody has to be able to talk to you to give you information. Sometimes you'll gain information by clearly just looking at your patient. If your patient is not breathing, that's giving you a lot of information. Something is wrong, they are critically sick, and you have to intervene—that's all the information in a situation like that that you need in order to intervene. You understand you have to start treatment for the patient. But you didn't know that, prior to having some information from your physical assessment revealing to you that the patient is not breathing. After gaining that information, you are now able to act. It needs to be understood that you have to have a certain amount of information in order to make a decision.

Now that being said, you can only make decisions based on the information you have. Another important principle is this: You must make the best decision you can based on the information in front of you at the time. It's easy to Monday-morning quarterback others after the fact. Keep this in mind during your self-reflection. Don't always judge yourself and your decisions based on the outcome of the patient. Sometimes patients decline and there is nothing you can do. You acted with the information you had, and that's what you're supposed to do. But be accountable for it.

Logic and Reason

When making decisions, you have to use logic and you have to act reasonably. These two definitions are hard to develop within the emergency or EMS system. Practicing EMS is an art form. You have to act and make decisions based on what a reasonable person would do in the situation that you're in, which is another aspect to consider when assessing your patients. Are your patients acting reasonably? Are they acting normal for what a reasonable person should be acting like given their situation?

If you try to act logically and rationally, it will be easier to reproduce. It will be more reliable. Irrational behavior and irrational decisions are based in lack of confidence and lack of decisiveness. If you start to make decisions irrationally or erratically, you have to step back and try to bring some reason and logic into the equation. You want to make decisions when you are clear minded. Not only does your patient have to be in a reasonable state of mind to make good decisions, this clarity of mind also filters to you as the paramedic.

One of the best ways to do this and develop this attribute is to stay in front of what is going on and don't react to a given situation. To stay reasonable and rational, you have to anticipate problems and situations that might arise. If you're able to anticipate whatever may occur, you're more able to rationally deal with them when they come up.

Gut Feeling or Intuition

Gut feeling and intuition sometimes come with experience. You can develop an intuition about what is going to happen with somebody if you have taken the time to interpret your experiences with other patients. This can serve you well if it is used properly. When that hair stands up on the back of your neck, you should pay attention.

Building and developing your intuition comes from reflecting upon other calls that you have run. You have to do this before the fact and after critical incidents, if you take the time to think through critical situations that you have encountered. Doing this will reinforce your intuition, and your intuition of future events will be sharper.

Intuition happens when you are able to recognize common themes or patterns with different types of patients. You will be able to better anticipate a patient's needs if you take the time to develop your intuition. Your intuition can best be developed by reflecting on critical incidents and trying to learn from them so that you can anticipate a patient's needs when you see a similar situation.

Objectivity

Objectivity is perhaps one of the most important aspects of decision-making. You have to remain objective to the information that you are interpreting. You have to be open and your mind has to be clear and able to digest the information that you're gathering for what it is. This goes for all aspects of life, not just EMS, but it is critically important in emergency situations. If you don't remain objective about information, you could make critical errors and mistakes. You can't put blinders on and make the information say something that it doesn't say. One of the most dangerous assumptions that paramedics can do is try to put something into a box it doesn't fit into. Paramedics sometimes try to make patients something that they're not.

Don't go into a call with a negative or preconceived notion of what is going on. You can start to anticipate based on dispatch information, but don't automatically downplay what could be happening. Remember, even your routine intoxicated party can have a serious medical or traumatic problem going on. A simple example—and something to routinely practice—is do not roll out the door and say to yourself, "Oh, this is going to be crap" or something similar. If you roll out the door on the alarm and say this to yourself, you are already disengaging mentally from the call, and it is more difficult to reengage if you encounter something more serious. Maintain your professionalism. Be ready for the unexpected. Do not disengage. Stay objective. You have to allow for every single call to have its own pieces of information that you have to gather.

In order to make a decision, you have to be objective. One of the biggest problems that can affect your decision-making is if you allow your personal opinions (emotions) to dictate what your decision is going to be. You have to allow the information to interpret itself so that you can make a good decision. You want to be careful to present yourself with the ability to digest whatever information comes your way. You have to be mentally capable of digesting information that you may not want to see or hear. Sometimes this information is critical, and sometimes it's not, but you still need to digest it appropriately and not allow it to be dictated by some other personal emotion.

Understand the difference between objective and subjective. Subjective is based on someone's idea or what someone is telling you. Objective information as it pertains to patient care is going to be verifiable findings such as a laceration to the head. That's an objective finding. If you approach patient care with an objective understanding in an objective approach, you're going to be able to take care of your patient better.

Now, hold on for this one because it's a bit thought provoking: You may base a treatment plan on what the patient is subjectively telling you, but you must remain objective in your interpretation of the information. Wow, that *was* a big one. For example, a patient might tell you that they have abdominal pain (subjective). After your exam you find no objective findings to verify why the patient might be having abdominal pain (objective). This does not mean the patient is not having pain. All it means is that you don't see tenderness, rigidity, or distention. But you are still basing your treatment plan on a subjective abdominal pain complaint.

This goes beyond just patient care but also allows you to not get burned out. We truly believe that one of the contributing factors to burnout is not from running lots of calls, but because you become personally invested—whether it's emotionally, politically, religiously, or whatever the investment is with the calls. This causes you to be stressed and invested in a situation that makes you fatigued emotionally. There's really no need for this. If you approach every patient regardless of their situation and circumstances objectively and try to treat each person individually about what's going on specifically with them, it will help you have longevity.

When you start to involve your own emotional, political, or other motivated factors to make decisions, your judgment will be clouded. You can't allow these emotions to cloud your judgment because sooner or later it will bite you in the rear. It's not appropriate for your patients and for the community that you serve to bring your own emotion into the room and your own political ideology into the realm of their specific patient care in an emergency situation. Your job is to treat, manage, and take care of the person in front of you. If you do this, you'll feel less stress and not make yourself vulnerable to burnout.

We're not saying that you should not get invested with your patient. You should invest yourself in patient care, but don't become personally invested in the political, socioeconomic, or emotional situation that people find themselves in. Don't invest yourself in trying to change or improve someone's political ideology because of what you believe. Just take care of your patient. For example, the patient who is a repeat victim of assault that refuses to leave their violent circumstances. Treat their injuries and give them all the resources you can to help them get out of the situation they are in. But do not become personally burdened by the patient not leaving. This will cause you to burn out quickly and can develop a future lack of empathy with other patients in the same situation. This logic comes back to what we previously discussed as understanding humility and understanding that you could be in a similar situation if it weren't for certain circumstances and people in your life.

Personal Factors That Cloud Your Judgment

What goes hand-in-hand with objectivity is your ability to not allow outside influences to affect your decision. This doesn't mean that you shouldn't be open to other people's interpretation of information or other people's ideas of what should take place and what you should do for a patient. You have to be careful of other factors you take into consideration.

There's a wide variety of these factors. Certain factors cause people to make poor choices and poor decisions. Do you think about workload? Do you think about how many patients you have or a car accident? Do you think about the paperwork incurred by having more patients? These questions could be summed up by asking this: Do you consider workload when you're making a decision? This is a question you have to ask yourself.

If the answer to this is yes, then you need to rethink what you're doing. Your workload should not be a factor in whether or not you treat somebody. You should not factor into your decision whether it creates another patient care report or whether or not you have a ride into the hospital, if that's applicable to your agency. The act of writing a refusal versus making someone a patient—does this ever enter your mind?

We're not going to tell you that these considerations don't enter all of our minds at some point. But we try to make a conscious decision to treat, even if the thought of paperwork comes up. Because what you're doing is subconsciously trying to talk yourself out of making a good decision.

Everybody you come across doesn't have to be a patient that requires paperwork, or someone you have to write a patient care report on, or that you have to ride into the hospital with. The point is that you should not allow these factors to dictate to you what type of decision you make. If you consider these factors into your decision-making, it's going to cause you to make worse decisions then you should be making. Just do the work. Part of the business is workload and paperwork. Don't allow factors such as these to drive you to make bad decisions.

When situations like this come up, instead of complaining or trying to get out of doing the work, you should look at this as an opportunity for you to practice discipline. You should think to yourself this is a good opportunity to exercise self-discipline. If you do this consistently, it will become second nature and sooner than you realize it will become the norm. Like we talked about before, it all comes back to being a professional. Are you or are you not a professional? Exercise self-discipline. This will make you a better paramedic, and it will make your community safer because of what you practice.

Consistency and Reliability

We've discussed consistency as it relates to a personal attribute of a professional paramedic, but when it comes to decision-making, consistency is also important. Consistency develops confidence and develops your understanding of what you're going to do in certain situations. Consistency helps you because it causes you to not start from square one with each patient. It allows you to recall what you've done with other patients that are similar to the ones that are in front of you. If you consistently treat people with the same plans and the same treatment methods and the same interventions, then you're not starting from the beginning with each individual patient. You can implement your treatment consistently and the task becomes easier.

The key to developing this approach, however, is through evaluating yourself and understanding why you're doing the interventions and why you implemented the treatment plan that you did for specific patients in certain situations. You have to take the time to evaluate yourself and reflect upon why you've done what you've done. This is the constant discipline of practicing self-reflection, which will produce self-growth and will help you develop a consistent approach to your treatment plan.

Consistency is also important in decision-making because it gives your team an idea of what's going to come next. Your team is better able to anticipate what your needs are if you're consistent in your treatment plans and interventions.

Although your treatment plans and interventions are important, it's much more important to consistently treat your patients with dignity and respect. These two values will take you a long way. If you practice consistently treating people the way that you would want to be treated, your treatment plans will become easier. It will become easier to implement them and decide what to do.

The other benefit of consistency is reliability. What you're doing is developing treatment plans and interventions that you've consistently implemented, and so now you can rely on them. Your process becomes reliable because you know what has worked in the past. Your teammates can now rely on you to make good decisions because you've consistently made your decisions. You want to have reliable treatment plans because this routine causes you much less stress. And you can make critical decisions in critical situations.

Consider this when it comes to consistency and reliability. By practicing self-reflection, you will develop self-growth. The result will be your consistency, which in turn gives you confidence because your decision-making is more reliable. Is this picture becoming clear? Are you beginning to see the benefits of adopting the attributes and principles set forth in an integrated way? All of these practices build on and complement each other.

Methodical Approach

You want to be methodical in your decision-making. You can't be making decisions arbitrarily or whimsically. Do you want to understand why you're making the decisions that you're making. Something we stress in training is taking a methodical approach to understanding what caused you to make the decision that you made. What did you see that made you decide what to do? You want to take the time to break down the calls that you run with the people that you train so that you can be more methodical in your approach.

Go over the little steps so that the big things are much easier. You want to encourage others to develop their own method. Don't make people make the same decisions that you make. Instead, help them understand the decisions they have already made, which will help them develop the skills of the paramedic rapidly. Help them become their own paramedic. Help them develop their own methods and help them to understand what those methods are.

What goes hand-in-hand, of course, is making sure that their methods reach the desired goal and standard of patient care. The beauty is that you will also learn from them. For those who are not teaching yet or not instructed yet, take the time to reflect on what your own methods are. Try to come to the point where you can articulate why you do what you do. You're looking for what caused you to implement certain treatment plans. What are your trigger points that caused you to intervene on whatever patient you have? What are your trigger points for intubating a patient? What are your trigger points for CPAP in a patient? What are your trigger points for putting a tourniquet on?

Understand what your own methods are and understand what your own trigger points are so you can be more consistent and reliable. If you can articulate what your method is and why you use it, it can benefit the student by helping them understand the importance of developing their own internal methods.

Open to New Information

When making decisions, make sure that you remain in a state of mind that allows you to take on new information. One of the only constants that you can be sure of when taking care of patients is that things are going to change. You have to be able to identify and digest new information. You have to be open with your crew and other participants who are giving you new information that might affect your decision. You have to be receptive to the idea of new thoughts and different information that might be gathered.

When making your decisions and you begin to act, don't shut yourself off to new information that might come your way. You might get more information that causes you to change your treatment plan and that's okay. But you have to remain in a state of mind that allows you to be open to new information. For example, you are ventilating an unresponsive patient from a traffic accident with a BVM, and your partner then says, "Here is a syringe. Maybe we should try Narcan?" You then administer Narcan because of the new information gathered.

Flexibility

Flexibility is highly important when it comes to decision-making. Flexibility goes along with the ability to quickly gather and interpret new information. You cannot get so set in a specific treatment or idea that it doesn't allow you to change. As we've talked about before, change is about the only constant that you will encounter when it comes to prehospital medicine. You have to be flexible and change your treatment plans based on a patient presentation or changing conditions.

If you're not flexible, then you're not going to be able to adapt to what is happening to your patient. Flexibility allows you to be able to change something with your treatment plan when your current plan is not going as you expected. When you give somebody a medication or you implement certain treatments that don't have the desired effect that you wanted, or the effect that you thought was going to happen, you have to be flexible enough to change what you're doing.

Sometimes you will fix certain conditions with the patient and something else will come up. You have to be flexible. Flexibility goes hand-in-hand with anticipation. If you remain flexible with your treatments, you are better able to anticipate outcomes. If you remain flexible, then when the unthinkable happens or when one of your patients takes a turn for the worse, you're more easily able to adapt. You'll be better able to deal with a surprise and make decisions that will improve the patient outcome, rather than freeze and continue down the same treatment path.

Flexibility gives you the ability to not ignore what might be going on with the patient. Ignoring symptoms and ignoring injuries that one of your patients might have is extremely detrimental, and sometimes the symptoms crop up after you started the treatment plan. If you remain flexible, you'll be better prepared to deal with whatever happens and make good decisions and incorporate the new information into the broader idea of what your treatment plan is.

Flexibility is also important because variables that you cannot control will also change. Some of these variables include the weather, who your crew is for the day, the time of day, and sleep. You cannot control these variables, but if you remain flexible, you can be just as effective with your treatment plans. Don't become upset with your emergency system and how it is set up. Whether it is with EMTs or EMT IVs or other paramedics. Work with who you have and stay flexible.

If you become upset because you don't have anyone else around who can help with some of the interventions, then you start focusing your attention on that, rather than intervening for the patient. The other detrimental and more insidious problem is that you start to dismiss what your other teammates are capable of. Just because they cannot start an IV or push epinephrine, they are still extremely valuable to you. Flexibility allows you to have a proper mental attitude to deal with changes that are outside your control.

Flexibility will also impact your longevity. If you must do things your way and only your way in your career, you will burn out. Be flexible when the uncontrolled events occur. It will most certainly cause you less stress. Don't fret about what you can't control; try to master the things you can.

Outside Influence

Outside influences are extremely important when it comes to decision-making. While it is important to be open to other people's ideas and information, you have to balance that with making good decisions. You ultimately are responsible, and you ultimately need to own the decisions you make. That doesn't mean that other people can't have valuable insight into what might be going on with the patient or situation. But don't let someone else talk you into doing something that you know is inaccurate or detrimental to your given situation.

Always remember that your crew or your partner is going to be affected by the same factors that affect you. Amount of sleep, time of day, call volume, or whether or not they've eaten—all these variables will play a role in your crew's decision-making. It will also affect how they interact with you when it comes to engaging with you about what to do about a patient. While those things are valuable, you have to balance the consequences with what's best for your patient. Is it inaccurate or detrimental to your given situation? Always remember that you need to make decisions based on being a patient advocate.

Other outside influences that can be detrimental—and something you don't want to allow to affect you in a negative way—are bystanders or witnesses to a patient or to an emergency situation. While witness or bystander information could be important in developing a picture of what is taking place, make sure you balance that with making decisions based on patient advocacy and proper interpretation of what they're telling you.

Remember that you're the professional and they called you. Bystanders and witnesses may not understand how your guidelines work or how you operate in the prehospital setting. Just because a bystander or witness is telling you to go faster, or bandage something, or implement some treatment plan that they think they have an understanding of does not necessarily mean that you have to do that.

Engage those people in a respectful, professional manner and implement your treatment plan based on what you are deciding. Sometimes these situations can become extremely volatile and you have to remain professional, and you have to have situational awareness in order to properly interpret the information that they are giving you. Take in the information that witnesses and bystanders give you, but filter it so that you can make a good decision about what to do with your patient or emergency.

Another form of an outside influence that might affect your decision-making is weather. Sometimes weather will play a role, but try not to let it affect your treatment plan. As soon as your environment allows you to implement what you would normally do, you need to immediately implement it. For example, if a patient in a car accident is in trouble or is sick and it's raining or snowing, you still have to maintain the standard of care that you would normally maintain if the weather were not bad. If you have to move these patients quickly to an environment that allows you to assess them properly before you fully engage in a treatment plan, then do so. Do not bypass or make bad decisions with your treatment plan because you are cold or wet. You have to maintain professional standards and give every patient the standard of care.

Time of day is another outside factor to consider. Don't allow the time of day to dictate to you what your treatment plan is. Time of day should not matter. Whether it's night and you're tired or daytime and you're hot and busy, don't allow time to dictate and affect your decision-making process. You have to take each call individually as they come and not let these outside factors influence your decision-making.

Another outside influence to be careful of is number of calls. Just because you're busy, the call in front of you still demands your full attention. Just because you might be behind on reports and have lots of paperwork to catch up on, that call in front of you still requires your full attention. The patient does not care how many calls you have run. You cannot let your fatigue from running too many calls affect your decision-making. If these factors are starting to affect your decision-making, you need to recognize it and act accordingly.

For some of you, call volume may create sleep deprivation. Sleep deprivation is extremely detrimental to decision-making. You have to maintain an adequate amount of sleep in order to make good decisions. The public that you are serving is expecting your full attention and devotion to their emergency. Make sure that you are getting enough sleep, and that you are giving yourself time to rejuvenate. Healthy sleeping will also help with burnout fatigue.

Take steps to mitigate outside influence from affecting your decision-making.

Risk vs Reward

Analyzing risk versus reward is an ongoing process. Risk and reward must be constantly analyzed and evaluated. When making decisions, you have to understand what the risk is of the intervention or the decision that you're deciding to do. You have to take into account what decisions you're making and how they're going to change and affect the patient and the situation you're in.

Some decisions may be based on low risk or relatively low risk, but other decisions might be based on high risk. A simple example would be giving a medication like Zofran, which is low risk. Or not performing a needle decompression when you should, which would be high risk, because now you are affecting your patient dramatically. You have to understand how you are affecting the situation you're in. In order to make a good decision, you have to constantly weigh the risk versus reward. Does the reward of outcome outweigh the risk of side effects or a negative outcome?

So many variables can affect risk and reward as it relates to each individual patient that you encounter, which is why this analysis has to be done case by case. This doesn't mean that you can't use experience from other similar decisions to help you decide what to do, but you do have to recognize that each person reacts differently or has the potential to react differently to certain interventions. Just because something works one time does not always mean that it will work every time. This is why you have to be flexible. Analyzing risk versus reward is an ongoing process. You have to continually weigh the risks and rewards to make sure that you are providing the best possible patient care in the emergency in front of you, to the best of your ability.

Confidence

Many factors contribute to building your confidence. Some of these factors include experience and gaining an understanding of the method that you're trying to implement and your own thought process. You have to understand what your individual thought process is. Not everybody is the same, so as long as you come to the same basic conclusions, it's better for you to understand what your thought process is than to replicate someone else's.

There are many ways to do the exact same thing. You have to act with confidence though. You have to be able to trust your assessment skills and trust the knowledge that you've been taught. You have to trust that you are going to engage with the patient and in the situations that you find yourself in and make good decisions.

Confidence is part of being professional, and then taking ownership of the decisions that you make. It will build your confidence to know that whatever the outcome is, you're going to hold yourself accountable to it. The process gives you the freedom to be confident in what you are doing. This liberates you from having to dance around certain decisions that you make. You won't have to be apprehensive about a decision if you make decisions with ownership and confidence. If you enter a situation with the knowledge and mind-set that you will hold yourself accountable for whatever happens, you are liberated from indecision.

One of the best ways to build your confidence is to analyze the decisions that you have made and understand what those outcomes were and analyze why you made that decision in that given situation. Situations similar to that will crop up in your career, and the self-reflection will give you confidence to know that you've dealt with these issues in the past and made good decisions.

Confidence is also extremely important for your teammates. They have to know that you are confident in your skills, that you are confident in your knowledge, and that you're confident in your decision-making process. When you are not confident about what you're doing and you second-guess yourself in a critical situation, this leads to the inability to act, which causes distress in the team and can become contagious and difficult to overcome. You want your team to be confident in you so that they are able to confidently accomplish the tasks that you set forth for them. Critical calls will be more successful if your team is confident that you are capable of properly directing them.

The inability to act is a direct result from lack of confidence. In order to build your confidence, you have to take the time to understand why you make the decisions that you do in certain situations and analyze why they were good decisions or bad decisions. Own those decisions and then move forward. Lack of confidence also bleeds over to your patient care. Your patient and also your team will be able to identify your lack of confidence, which may cause them to become uneasy. If your patient is able to see that you are not acting confidently or that you are scared of the situation that you're in, you can cause the patient to become more stressed and could potentially cause more harm. Remember that you have to act like a professional even if you are scared. You will be concerned and anxious in certain situations, but you have to remain professional and act confidently and decisively.

Setting small goals to achieve will develop your confidence. Confidence is quickly built when you achieve small successes. Success is more easily measured if you have a predetermined goal that can be attributed to it. Develop this idea with small goals and small successes, and it will quickly allow you to develop bigger goals. The larger goals achieved will produce more confidence, and if you have clear goals, your success is much easier to measure. You will then know that you are making good decisions. If you want to make good decisions, start with the small things such as setting a goal to review the guidelines of one medication every single morning.

Just to reiterate, in order to build your confidence, you have to analyze and reflect upon different calls that you have run. You have to take the time to reflect on what worked, and what did not work, and why you made the decisions that you made. What did you see that led you to make the decisions that you made? If you take the time to reflect upon this, it will build your confidence because you are more quickly able to adapt to what your thought process is and what your decision-making process is. You will more quickly adapt to what interventions work with certain patients. You will get a better understanding of how to treat a wide variety of patients as well.

Analyze and Anticipate

To make good decisions, you have to think about or analyze the significance of the decision that you're going to make. How is the decision going to affect your patient or the situation that you are currently in? If you take the time to think ahead before you act, you will have more confidence that you are making a good decision. You will gain insight into whether or not you are making a good decision.

You want to try to anticipate the outcome of the decision you're making. You have to be able to anticipate what's going to happen when you perform certain interventions. If you're not planning ahead, you are only making decisions based on what you see and not considering what you're trying to change.

You're making decisions with the expectation of certain changes. Whenever we make decisions, we're trying to make decisions to affect some sort of change on whatever the situation is. You're going to be better at making decisions if you understand what changes are going to occur and what the expected outcome is based on what you are deciding to do. By adopting this approach, you are analyzing your decisions.

Anticipating and analyzing will also affect what the significance of that outcome is—meaning was it a major change in patient condition or a minor change? Analyzing what you did allows you to readdress something after a decision or intervention was done. You can't just make decisions arbitrarily or whimsically with no regard for what you're trying to accomplish. You have to keep a larger picture in mind and understand the broad picture of what you're trying to change and what you're trying to accomplish, and consider the significance of those decisions and how you're trying to implement your overall patient care and treatment plan.

You also have to analyze, expect, and understand potential side effects or other potential problems with interventions and decisions that you make. If you decide to go down a certain route, you have to understand what the potential problems are with going down that route. If you're not anticipating and preparing yourself for negative outcomes of decisions that you've made, you're going to be behind the eight ball when the patient has a negative reaction to a decision that you've made regarding the treatment plan or intervention. You want to try to set yourself up for success and mitigate potential problems and potential side effects by anticipating and analyzing the decisions you're making and how they're going to affect your patient and what the potential problems are.

A simple example of this would be after deciding to RSI (rapid sequence intubation) a patient, analyze the potential for problems and anticipate them. Plan for the best but prepare for the worst. Plan on being able to quickly intubate the patient and ventilate them, however, have your contingencies ready. Where are your basic airway supplies? Do you have your rescue airway prepared? Where is your cric kit? This is a simple example of anticipation through analyzing your decision to RSI your patient.

Analyzing will allow you to stay in front of problems that occur. It also allows for easier flexibility and transitions when something goes bad. If you are anticipating problems happening or side effects that could occur, you won't be caught off guard when those things do occur and you're much more easily able to switch gears and change the course of action and make a different decision based on what you're looking at. You are better able to start a different treatment plan that might be better suited for your patient.

If you don't anticipate problems and potential side effects, then when bad things happen, you're going to be caught off guard. You may become nervous, and then poor planning may affect your ability to act. Unanticipated problems hinder your development of confidence. They make it harder for you to build confidence in the decisions that you make. You can start to feel as if you're not accomplishing the goals you want. You feel like you are not being successful, and every action you're taking has a negative outcome, or an outcome that you didn't see coming.

If you anticipate and understand when those problems are going to happen, and why those problems are happening, you'll have confidence that you're able to fix those problems and change the course of action and intervene. You cannot make decisions without understanding the potential consequences of the decisions you are making. You have to take into account the consequences of your actions and the consequences to your patient or situation that your decision is going to affect. You do this by analyzing your decisions.

Additionally, you have to anticipate your need for follow-on procedures. You have to understand what your protocols or guidelines are, and what they require of you. A couple examples of this would be utilizing capnography for intubated patients or patients that you have given pain medications to, or subsequent 12 leads post–cardiac arrest or multiple 12 leads in order to get a better picture of your patient's status. If you're not anticipating the needs for follow-on procedures that some of your decisions will require of you, you're not looking at the whole picture in the whole treatment plan that you were trying to integrate. You're only doing half of the treatment that is required of you, which causes you to have a lack of understanding of the decisions that you have made.

If you decide to intubate somebody and you don't anticipate having to give them capnography and what that entails for you and for the patient, it reveals that you are not understanding fully the significance of the procedures that you are deciding to do. It also reveals that you are not analyzing your decision and anticipating the other interventions that must be done as well as a result of your decision.

Some of the decisions you make will require more work. Like we've talked about before, you should not allow the idea of more work to affect what your decision is. You have to understand that and anticipate that some of the interventions you do will automatically require more work from you. Analyzing and anticipating that you may have more work from your decision gives you better clarity on why you are performing the procedures that you are performing, and the significance of those procedures, and the potential problems and side effects of those procedures.

Analyze What You Have Done

One simple tool that will help you develop your decision-making process that seems to be obvious—but for some people it is not so obvious—is to analyze what you have done. Earlier we talked about self-reflection and what you did on certain calls, and then general reflection about what the call was.

You have to analyze the information that you gathered during the incident and how you interpreted it and what your treatment plan was. You need to take the time to understand why you came to the conclusion that you did. This begins with small things. This begins with deciding whether or not to do 12 leads on a patient with your cardiac monitor, or deciding whether to start an IV and give a patient Zofran because they're feeling nauseated. If you can analyze and understand how you gathered your information and what that information meant to you, and why it led you down a certain path to decide other interventions, you develop good habits and effective decision-making processes. When you start with the little things, then you can move on to the bigger things, which makes big decisions much easier. Because you start small to slowly develop a process, you use that to make a decision the same way for much more difficult items.

Take time to think about your mistakes. You are going to make mistakes, and that's expected. You have to know ahead of time that mistakes are going to be made. You have to do the best you can to mitigate these mistakes so they don't happen often and don't cause negligence or they don't cause you to treat the patient below the standard of care. You have to think about your mistakes, but don't dwell on them. Don't cause your mistakes to become so overwhelming that you can't move forward. You have to come to a conclusion and resolve on why you made the mistake and what information you gathered that caused you to make the decision that you made and why it was a mistake.

You have to use the same process with mistakes that you use with your successes to understand the information gathered, why you interpreted it a certain way, and if the decision was good or bad. You have to take the opportunity to learn from your mistakes. Mistakes can cause you to become unsure of yourself and lose confidence. You have to look at mistakes as opportunities. In other words, mistakes are good opportunities for your development and growth. You'll learn from mistakes better than you learn from successes. You have to have the mind-set of learning what *not* to do and that what not to do is just as important as learning what *to* do.

One of the biggest factors with mistakes is that you have to allow yourself to be open to criticism. Allow people to critique you, and allow other paramedics and your physician advisors and your medical divisions to critique what you've done, and allow them to help you grow. When you make a mistake, you need to take the time to understand why you made it so that you can articulate it to the doctors or to your physician advisors.

When you clearly understand why you did what you did and you're confident in why that decision was made, it allows you to be much more open for critique. Don't always be on the defensive and don't always defend positions and treatment plans that you know to be wrong when there's a better way or when someone is trying to give you advice on what to do better next time. Use these moments as opportunities. Even if the people that you are discussing your mistakes with are not prone to giving you constructive criticism, use that and come with the attitude that you're going to get something out of it. Don't be so arrogant to believe that you know how to handle every single situation that will arise and that you will never need input from somebody else.

We continue to come back to this idea of professionalism and ownership. Taking ownership of your mistakes liberates you from having to make excuses. When you are liberated from having to make excuses, you are now open to growth. The key to growth is to conduct yourself with a professional attitude and be open to criticism and take ownership for the mistakes that you make.

Be Assertive

Being assertive goes hand-in-hand with proper communication. You have to communicate what your intentions are with your team and other agencies that might be involved with your patient or scene. In an emergency situation someone has to lead and take charge of the chaos that is surrounding them, and in many instances this is the job of the paramedic. You have to take charge of the scene if that's what your role is and be assertive in stepping into that role. In the absence of leadership, leadership will rise. Someone will lead.

Being assertive is extremely important in your decision-making process. But what does this actually mean? Being assertive is having confidence in your decisions and having a vision for how to get there. Then, after being confident in what you want to accomplish and understanding how you are going to do it, properly communicate to your teammates and implement your vision. Say your patient can't walk and is stranded upstairs. Your vision for getting them to the ambulance is to get a stair chair and carry the patient downstairs and then lift them onto the cot. You can then load them safely into the ambulance. You must clearly inform your teammates of your vision for accomplishing the task of getting the patient down the stairs.

Then after you take charge, properly communicate to your team what your vision is for patient care, what your treatment plan is, or what your vision is to mitigate an emergency situation, and how you want your team members to help you accomplish that vision. Being assertive does not mean being overly aggressive and dismissive. While being assertive, you still have to be open to other people's information and ideas. You cannot be closed-minded because you are being so aggressive with your treatment that you are now unable to realize other people's ideas have value for what might be going on. Being assertive is understanding that you are going to take responsibility for your actions.

Not deciding to act is a decision. Sometimes it's the right decision because somebody might not need a procedure or an intervention performed. However, sometimes the decision to not act is going to negatively affect your patient outcome. Sometimes not acting is the right decision but sometimes it's not. You have to be able to differentiate between the two and understand when they are both appropriate.

Being assertive also relates to your responsibility to set a proper tone for the situation. This assertiveness allows others to have confidence in the chaos or the emergency. This assertiveness is a direct reflection of your ability to lead people. When others see an assertive leader, they quickly follow. This assertive mentality produces success because there is no longer hesitation on the part of the team. They have full confidence in your ability to lead.

Being assertive also improves your rapport with your patient. Your patient care cannot be filled with hesitation and self-doubt. Your patient needs to be confident in your decisions. This comes from your assertive direction of others and your command of the scene or situation. Your leadership abilities are on display, so be confident in your decisions and earn the confidence of those you are leading.

Knowledge or Action

Finally we come to the crux of the matter. What is more important? Knowledge and information or action? Now obviously a base knowledge is important to have and will drive your action, but we would argue that knowledge is not the fundamental characteristic that makes a good paramedic. In fact we say that knowledge plays very little importance on how successful a paramedic is.

We'll be the first to admit that a lot of information in medicine and emergency medicine is over our heads and we don't understand. But the beautiful thing about emergency medicine in the field is that none of that is as important as taking definitive action on a critical patient. If you have a basic understanding of what you learned in paramedic school and a basic understanding of disease processes and anatomy and physiology, then you can use that understanding to make good decisions and act.

We would also argue that action is the most important aspect of being a good paramedic. You can sit back all day long and analyze what might be going on with the patient because you have so much knowledge you're attempting to specifically diagnose a certain issue rather than acting on what the patient is presenting. If you are the type of person who is able to retain all the information that you read and you are able to gather vast amounts of knowledge of medicine and understanding of medicine, then that is fantastic, but don't let that delay your action.

One of the other actions you must do to be successful especially if you have vast amounts of understanding is to be humble about your understanding and knowledge and pass it along to others in a gentle manner. Don't be boastful about how much knowledge you have. At the end of the day, everybody gets the patient to the hospital, and we would argue that the one who acts quicker on basic knowledge and acts more definitively is doing the patient better service than someone who sits back and tries to analyze every minute detail of what might be going on with the patient.

We're not saying that you have to overlook differential diagnoses and that you shouldn't have an open mind to many different disease processes that might be going on with the patient. What we're saying is don't let that delay your action. You have to intervene with people in critical situations. While you're thinking about what's going on with the patient, start interventions. Be more cognizant of what your scope of practice is and what problems you have the ability to mitigate.

An example: Don't be consumed with whether your patient has appendicitis, pancreatitis, or cholecystitis and then overlook the fact that they are septic. You need to recognize these possibilities and understand the basic knowledge of what might be causing those concerns and then act appropriately. Then you can intervene and conduct your proper interventions based on your protocols and notify your incoming hospital of what is going on with the patient and how they are presenting.

It's much more beneficial for your patient in the field for you to recognize sepsis rather than recognize appendicitis specifically.

Don't become consumed with your understanding and knowledge that you overlook the overall picture and the overall health of your patient. The hospital has much more capabilities and has the diagnostic tools to really zero in on what might be going on with the patient. Now all of this being said, again let us reiterate: If you can understand and diagnose these differential diagnoses in the field, that is fantastic, but don't let that thought process and your thinking through all the different possibilities that might be going on delay your interventions. Hopefully you gather knowledge throughout your career and gather understanding and experiences so that you are able to think through these possibilities simultaneously while you act and have working diagnoses and working differentials for what might be going on.

Being confident in your understanding and being confident in the knowledge that you do have will give you the ability to act. You have to be harmonious with your action and understanding. You can be intervening with people while you are thinking about what might be going on. Don't become consumed in your thoughts about which disease process that you're not intervening on for somebody who can't breathe, has an irregular heartbeat, or is hemorrhaging. You have to act.

Knowledge and information that you gain is developed by study and through paramedic school. This is important to your fundamental understanding of medicine. But if you do not know how to properly interpret the information that you are gathering from your patient, your knowledge will be useless. If you can't recognize what the patient is presenting and how that relates to your understanding of medicine and then how that relates to your taking action and intervening, then your knowledge is useless.

One of the best tools that you can develop as a paramedic is your listening skills. You have to allow the patient to tell you what's going on so that you can properly interpret, through your lens of understanding medicine, what might be going on and then let that information drive your action and intervention. In some cases too much knowledge for some people can be a crutch. If you're taking too much time to chase too many different routes or you are delayed and frozen with inaction and you're not intervening because you're thinking about too many different possibilities, the options can be a crutch. Just remember that information itself is useless if it is not properly applied.

Section III

Teaching Others

7

The Real Truth

Clear the Air

Okay, let's clear the air. Let's just get right down to the nitty-gritty and put everything on the table. Let's say what needs to be said so there's no misunderstanding. Here it goes. Nobody cares how great you think you are. Nobody!

This is important when it comes to precepting (teaching others), and it's also important when it comes to paramedicine in general. This topic has already been discussed as it relates to the characteristic of humility and being a professional paramedic. You can't be egotistical and humble at the same time; they are diametrically opposed to one another. The expression of your personal ego is something that needs to be put aside after attaining your paramedic and certainly before assuming the role of a preceptor. Nobody cares how smart you think you are. Not your student, not your friends, not your spouse, not your coworkers, and certainly not your patient.

Don't misunderstand. Your being a skilled paramedic is something that is internalized with your ability to express yourself in a professional manner. It comes from your confidence in your own skill set that is on open display. It's about action, not talking about how much you know. Professional paramedics don't rant arrogantly about how great they are or how great they think they are. Their actions speak for themselves. Pridefulness should not be found in the realm of paramedicine, and it certainly should not be found in the realm of precepting. If you are truly that talented and knowledgeable, people will recognize it by your professionalism and ownership, not by your regurgitation of knowledge.

All ego does is get in the way of developing a new paramedic. A preceptor's ego is going to inhibit the preceptee's (student's) ability to learn. If all you're doing is constantly demonstrating your superior knowledge or your superior skill set, or superior assessments, or superior report writing, you're going to create an environment of tension. Your preceptee is not going to respond to you favorably if you're constantly demonstrating your superiority. Ego must be in check.

Let's keep something else in mind here, and this is an extremely important and often forgotten principle both in leadership in general and also in paramedicine. This principle is that you as the preceptor are there for the preceptee. You are there for them, not them for you. That's something you have to keep in mind as an evaluator. If you're not willing to subject yourself and put yourself in a position of servitude so that you can make them better, you shouldn't be a preceptor.

While developing this idea, let us revisit the attribute of self-reflection. If you're truly going to be honest with yourself and trying to become a better paramedic, it will manifest in ways that will help to develop the new paramedic. If you are constantly trying to become better yourself, that quality will bleed over into your preceptee. If you think that you're already the greatest, you have nowhere else to go, there is no room for self-growth.

Let's be honest, you are not the best paramedic. You are not the most knowledgeable. You are not the most informed. You haven't run all the alarms. You don't know everything. You too can learn a thing or two. You are always able to glean more insight into a call or develop a thought process more and become a better paramedic.

Something else that's important to remember as it relates to your ego and the preceptor role is this: Your student might actually teach you something. The most that we've ever learned about being a paramedic was when having to instruct, mentor, or teach somebody else how to do the job. That's when we learned the most. Not beforehand, but after going through a moment of instructing or being responsible for teaching somebody else, that's when you can develop yourself exponentially as a paramedic.

It's important to understand that you are responsible for instructing the new paramedic and also for developing them professionally. This involves specifically leaving your ego out of the way because they will latch on to the egotistical megalomania that has overwhelmed some paramedics. If you're one of those who thinks you're so great and has assumed the identity of a paragod, that's going to bleed over into your new paramedic, and you're just perpetuating the problem.

Your students and your new paramedics are going to come to you with all sorts of backgrounds. We have touched on this before but will bring it up again and address it quickly. Your students are going to have all sorts of different life experiences, expectations, and requirements. Don't for one second think that through all of these different life experiences and different ways of doing things you can't glean some new knowledge, or new ways to better apply your own knowledge. Don't be so egotistical and self-absorbed that you think your student can't teach you something. Some of the greatest success is from multiple people putting their minds together to solve a problem.

[Sam's story] I recall an example where a man was stuck with his foot in the mud. Everybody was trying to figure out how to get this man's foot out of the mud. They would dig and dig trying to get it out. They tried all of the rescue techniques. And at the end of the day the new firefighter came in and said, "Oh, let me show you how to get his foot out. Let me show you how to do this." They simply took a hose, stuck it in the mud next to his foot, and turned on the water. His foot popped right out. And this is after hours of a man's foot being stuck in the mud. Not to mention hours of people who are extremely competent in their ability to rescue. But all this does is demonstrate that you can learn from other people all the time.

Don't become someone who thinks that you're so good at your job and you're so egotistical that nobody else is going to teach you anything. That nobody else is going to come and inform you. Allow that humility to take you so that you are in a position where you can receive new knowledge or instruction so that you yourself can become a better paramedic. This concept is extremely important when it comes to precepting. Don't pass on your egotistical, self-absorbed qualities to your new student or your new paramedic. Let's stop the process and begin acting as professionals.

One final thought, and this is the thought that has nothing to do with medicine. But it has everything to do with the ego. Getting rid of your ego is one of the most important acts you can do in your life. Getting rid of your ego and self-absorbed expressions transcends the world of paramedicine; it transcends the professional world. You need to adopt an attitude of service to your fellow man. This advice specifically relates to paramedicine, but can easily be adopted in your personal life. If we all adopted an attitude in which we continually mean to serve others instead of adopting an attitude by which we should be served, we would all be better off. Food for thought.

Set the Professional Tone

Setting the tone for all aspects of your life and living with intention is extremely important. Nothing is different here as it pertains to the preceptor. We've talked about setting the tone when it comes to beginning a call or starting off to a scene or responding to an alarm. But now we will briefly discuss setting the tone as it relates to being a preceptor.

Setting the tone does not begin with your student or your new paramedic. Setting the tone begins with you as the preceptor. You are the example. You are going to dictate how the internship or precepting is going to begin. And what better place to start with than you. This begins with you and your attitude and willingness to being a consummate professional. You now are not only responsible for your own professionalism, but in some ways you're going to mold and impact the professionalism of others. This is a huge responsibility. Now it's come to the point where your actions, your mannerisms, your ways of expressing what is and what is not as important, and how you conduct yourself in a professional way is going to rub off on your preceptee or the new paramedic. They're now going to look at you as a role model.

They'll mimic your medicine; they will mimic your abilities to assess patients; they'll mimic the way you conduct yourself as a professional. Let's keep in mind that being the professional is probably the most important part of this entire scope. Because everybody can develop their own ways of doing things and administering patient care, yet without any professionalism, everything else will always be lacking. If you don't conduct yourself in a professional manner, nobody will follow you, nobody will ever trust you, nobody will ever want to mimic you, nobody will ever care how well you can perform skills if you don't do it in a professional manner.

Now this is where you have to truly ask yourself if you are a professional. *Do I conduct myself in a professional way?* These are simple questions that you have to ask yourself before even entertaining the idea of training someone else.

If you're the one who comes to work and lacks the willingness to do your job, then being a preceptor is probably not for you. If you're the one who comes to work every day with a dirty uniform, ungroomed and unclean. If you're the one who comes to work with a bad attitude and a lack of willingness to do your job, then being a preceptor is probably not for you.

Being a preceptor goes part and parcel with being a consummate professional. You now are not only a representative of what it means to be a good paramedic, you're also a representative of the organization you work for. They have now placed the responsibility of training others and bringing them up within your organization. You're no longer just representing yourself. You are now representing the organization you work for. They have placed that responsibility on you to train people and bring them up within that discipline.

You must conduct yourself in a professional way. This begins with your attitude when you wake up in the morning and when you go to work. This begins with when you walk in the door to your fire station or go to your ambulance and you begin to check out your equipment. It begins with your morning conversations with the off-going crew. Are you a positive force within the job, or a negative one? Do you set a positive tone?

Some of the characteristics that have been discussed are going to come up again especially when it comes to setting the tone in your role as a preceptor. Accountability is one that really stands out. Accountability is extremely important. You as a preceptor are going to be responsible for holding somebody else accountable. Accountability goes hand-in-hand with professionalism. You now will be accountable for your preceptee or your new paramedic. You are going to hold them accountable for their actions, so you must hold yourself accountable for yours. If you're going to hold somebody else to their actions, you better be willing to hold yourself accountable for your actions. You're accountable to yourself now and you're further accountable for the preceptee, and also you are more accountable to the organization that you are working for.

Accountability takes on an entirely new scope. We are no longer in the realm of worrying about yourself. Now you have to worry about somebody else and their actions and their role. You will be held accountable for anything that you do or don't do as it relates to training your preceptee. You can't be signing off on their ability to perform on a cardiac arrest when you haven't witnessed them perform on a cardiac arrest. If they become cleared of their field instruction and they totally botch a cardiac arrest, it comes back to you and your training. You can't say that they're able to perform tasks and skills that you're not sure of. You can't say they embody these specific characteristics that are important to being a paramedic if you haven't witnessed them. You'll be held accountable for what you write off and what you pencil whip or whatever sort of process or procedure your organization requires of the preceptor. Keep that in mind as you begin your journey in the preceptor role.

This doesn't mean that you have to evaluate your trainee running every single type of call that is possible. But it does mean that you are accountable for their understanding and thought process. You are responsible for ensuring that the trainee can make good decisions.

We've discussed integrity at length earlier, but as it pertains to the role of a preceptor, it's incredibly important. Your integrity will be called into question. If you are going to be a preceptor, your integrity cannot waiver. You must be a person of integrity. You cannot allow for falsehoods and dishonesty to creep up within the internship. Because if you do, you will pass that sort of attitude on to your preceptee, and it will become a cancer within the environment of practicing paramedicine. It will do nothing but harm the entire profession. You have to be a person of integrity, and you have to be willing to be responsible for what does and does not happen on your scenes.

Yes, your integrity will be challenged, and you will have to answer for what your student does or does not do. This is where you must set the professional example and instill a sense of integrity within your preceptee. This goes along with accountability. Setting the proper tone by displaying the attributes of integrity and accountability is essential.

Now we must discuss the importance of having a good work ethic. If you don't have a good work ethic, you have no business being a preceptor. None. A good work ethic includes being present and being willing to observe and evaluate your preceptee. If you don't have a good work ethic and you're not willing to work hard for the things that you are accountable for, what gives anybody any confidence that you're willing to work hard for those things when it's somebody else's responsibility? If you haven't instilled a good work ethic within yourself, you have no business being a preceptor.

If you're the one showing up to work late, if you're the one always lacking on reports, if you're always complaining about the job, if you're always concerned about how everybody else is conducting themselves, this is a problem. You need to reel it in and focus on your own personal work ethic. This is the time to be consumed with being a professional paramedic. If you don't have a good work ethic, don't become a preceptor yet.

Having a good work ethic is a trait that must be practiced. You don't just wake up and decide to have one. You must practice these habits. You have to force yourself to go through your medications, to do your daily checks, to write a good report, to put on a clean and neat uniform, to have a good attitude and not talk unprofessionally about everybody else. These are simple habits that must be worked on in order for you to have a good work ethic.

Conversely, having a good work ethic will be noticed by your organization and by your peers. Having a good work ethic is going to drive new paramedics to you. They're going to want to precept with you because they understand the importance of these skills. Your organization will witness your good work ethic and will send people to you, and they will willingly give you that responsibility. Having a good work ethic is extremely important when it comes to setting the proper tone as a preceptor. A brief side note here, even if your agency doesn't want you to train others, you should continue to strive for a good work ethic. You should work hard for yourself first.

We briefly discussed three attributes that are critically important to professionalism and especially with respect to the role of a preceptor. These attributes are essential when setting the proper tone for the internship with your preceptee. Within the role of a preceptor, professionalism is paramount. And in order to have professionalism and be professional, these three characteristics are vitally important to have. These characteristics of accountability, integrity, and work ethic are difficult to obtain. They are not easy to maintain. These characteristics require constant attention. They require constant work and self-reflection. You have to have an internal motivation to be a consummate professional. There will be times where you want to drop the ball and take the easy way out. When you don't want to be accountable for something that was small or seemingly minuscule but you must. If you're not willing to be accountable or you're not a person of integrity with the small things, you'll never be someone who is accountable for the big things. If you are unwilling to do what's right when it has tiny consequences, where is the confidence that you're willing to do what's right when the ramifications are enormous? You have to work on these things constantly.

If you practice these attributes consistently, they will become habitual. When traits like these become habitual, they no longer require as much energy from you to maintain. It is then integrated into your thought process and integrated into your practice.

You now are the preceptor. You have demonstrated these characteristics that embody professionalism. You now must be a consummate professional, because you will be responsible for those you train. It's a great privilege to be a preceptor. Just remember, be a professional and set the proper tone.

8

Ready to Teach?

Role of the Preceptor

We now must look at defining the role of the preceptor. It's easy to ascribe someone that position or give them that sort of role, but what does preceptor really mean? There's much more to being a preceptor than being a paramedic who is full of knowledge or abilities and skills.

Being a good preceptor has surprisingly little to do with your own ability to regurgitate information that you've read out of a book or that you've gleaned from an article. Being a good preceptor also doesn't necessarily require you to have more experience and general knowledge than somebody else. Being a good preceptor fundamentally requires you to be able to manage and lead people, to be able to teach someone how to apply their knowledge. When we think about determining whether or not somebody should be a preceptor, we look at other paramedics and ask if they will do a good job.

But we must ask ourselves why? Why will that person be a good preceptor? If the answer is because they've been a paramedic for a long time or they know lots of things or they've got so much experience, that doesn't necessarily mean they will be a good preceptor. A preceptor's primary role and fundamental responsibility is to teach the new paramedic to apply the knowledge that they've already gained. These new paramedics coming through and interning with you, the preceptor, have already demonstrated their ability to regurgitate information. They've already demonstrated their core competence in all of the various areas and skills that are needed to be a paramedic. They've already been through the classroom instruction on cardiology, IV medication administration, pharmacology, anatomy and physiology, pathophysiology, and everything else.

They have been taught the skills of starting IVs, putting on EKGs, intubating, and other vital skills needed to be a paramedic. All of these skills and this knowledge have been tested. That's why they've been through the school. They went to school, to the classroom, to learn the base foundational knowledge of what it takes to be a paramedic.

Learning never stops. That's a given. Once the foundation is laid and the basics learned, now the new paramedics can begin to intern with you. You must allow them to apply that knowledge and begin to guide their decision-making. It's not your job as a preceptor to teach them cardiology or pharmacology or whatever discipline. If they are truly deficient in knowing how to read a 12 lead, they may need some remedial training. This doesn't mean you don't address these disciplines as they come up, but it shouldn't be your focus. Your primary concern should be teaching them to apply the concepts they have already learned.

This is much easier said than done. Teaching somebody to apply something is much more difficult than teaching somebody something. It takes much more skill and time to teach the application of knowledge than to just teach the knowledge itself. It's not difficult to teach the basic skills of RSI, or to teach the basic skills of how to intubate, or how to physically begin an IV. However, that's the difference between a paramedic and everybody else—the paramedic must understand when and why to do those procedures.

It's not good enough to simply know how to perform a skill. The paramedic must understand why intubating this person is appropriate, why starting the IV is appropriate, or why the patient needs an EKG. The new paramedic coming to you is going to have a brand new tool box, shiny and pristine, ready to go to work. They're going to have all these new tools that they want to use and newly acquired knowledge of how to use those tools, but you're going to have to mentor them in their understanding of *why* they use them and *when* they use them. You have to develop their application of their new tools.

Many different people are going to come to you for training. Sometimes it is a revolving door. You will see so many different skill sets and abilities. Not to mention the many different places that they come from and life experiences they bring to the table. You're going to have to sift through all of these different variables and figure out how to get your students to apply their knowledge specifically. You can't easily define how to make every single person apply the knowledge that they have. That's the difference, because every paramedic will have their own way of operating. That's the understanding that the preceptor must have.

It's difficult to sit down and write an algorithm for every single person who is going to come through and precepts with you on how to apply the knowledge they have. Because everybody's going to come to you with a different learning style, a different way of applying things, so you have to be able to adapt to them. You shouldn't be requiring them to adapt to you. You need to figure out how they function, how they work, how they think, what they're thinking about and why, so that you can help them guide their own decision-making process. You can't mandate that they do things exactly like you. You have the way that you do things, which is different than everybody else's. We all have our own styles, yet we all have a goal at the end, and guidelines that we must stay within and parameters that we can't deviate from, but getting to the end is the goal.

Getting there can look much different from paramedic to paramedic. You can't go on a chest pain patient and go through some algorithm of how to teach that paramedic how to apply the knowledge they have about a chest pain patient. You have to mentor them in developing a consistent, methodical approach to those chest pain patients.

This is your role as preceptor. By your giving them the liberty to develop their own approach, they are also learning how to properly make decisions. They are learning how they make decisions. The variables in the world of paramedicine are incalculable. You will never know it all, but if you know how to make good decisions, it doesn't matter what you encounter. You will always be prepared because you have a consistent approach. Mentorship starts here, as you must begin to develop your students' consistent, methodical decision-making.

If you don't apply this principle in precepting, all you're doing is teaching them what your system is. You're not allowing them to develop their own system; you're not allowing them to figure out how they're going to apply their knowledge. This is difficult to do because, on the one hand, you have to maintain a high standard of practicing medicine and being a paramedic, but, on the other hand, you have to allow them to develop their own systematic approach to the work. You have to allow them to develop their own methods.

It's your job, however, as the preceptor to maintain a high level of patient care and be able to treat people properly and safely while simultaneously allowing somebody else to do it their way. You can't mandate them to do it your way. Now with that said, when things aren't going well or when somebody's treating a patient inappropriately, that's when you have to step in. That's when you take over the call, and you can discuss why and when and how the reasons that led up to your taking over afterward. Rarely do you as a preceptor need to explain why you're taking over the call during the call itself. Feedback should be done in a more private setting where you don't berate the paramedic student publicly, not to mention losing the trust of the patient. Just to make it clear, you should not berate them privately either. You should mentor them.

All of this discussion has described an important principle that you as a preceptor must have: be a master at adaptation. You should be able to adapt to changing environments, changing calls, changing differential diagnoses, changing attitude, changing dispositions on scene, changing levels of care, changing treatment plans, changing implementations of treatment plans—all of the different concepts that generally a paramedic must have, you have to be a master at it. If you're a person who is so nervous on scene when things aren't going well or events aren't going exactly how you foresaw them, the responsibility of being a preceptor is not yours; you have not yet mastered the necessary quality of being adaptive. You're not somebody who can teach somebody else if you can't adapt to certain changes.

If you haven't already figured it out, you need to be reading the earlier sections of this book and begin by implementing those plans in your practice of medicine. You need to be figuring out your own self-growth and having some self-reflection on whether or not those attributes are in your repertoire or not. You need to determine what your decision-making is actually like. You have to be able to adapt to your students' needs and their abilities, and their knowledge and their application of it. If you can't adapt to situations, you have no business being a preceptor. Your student doesn't care how great you think you are or how many books you read. Their only concern is learning about how they're going to apply their knowledge. That's your job.

Keep in mind it is perfectly fine to not be a preceptor. There are a multitude of excellent paramedics in this country and around the world that are not responsible for training others. It is okay to not take on that responsibility. In fact it is admirable to be able to recognize that you might not have those specific desires. However, you should still strive to be the professional paramedic the public deserves.

So now we've come to the understanding that you must allow the new paramedic to form their own decisions and their own decision-making process. We've discussed the need for the preceptor to be willing to adapt to other ways of doing things and not be so rigid in their abilities to complete a call or assess a patient. But actually doing this is much more difficult than you might imagine. How is it that you actually do allow somebody to form their own decision-making processes? As stated before, it begins with your ability to adapt to your students' ways of doing things. You have to be willing to allow your student latitude when it comes to making decisions. You have to allow your student the latitude to make their own decisions. You have to give them the latitude to go down different pathways of questioning about differential diagnoses.

Remember there's a big difference between observing somebody assessing a patient and actually assessing a patient yourself. We've all had those preceptors or have witnessed those preceptors that stand over their student's shoulder and immediately direct the line of questioning. How does one develop their own abilities to assess somebody when they're only being directed specifically on what to say and when to say it? You have to give the student latitude to make their own decisions and develop their own differential diagnosis and treatment plans and you have to give them the latitude to implement the treatment plans. This is where your ability to adapt to a different way of doing things is crucial.

Understandably, we all work within specific guidelines. We're not saying that you allow your preceptee to go outside of those parameters or function in an unsafe way. What we're stressing is that you have to be willing to allow your student the same latitude for figuring out how to function within those parameters. This may mean that you have to step in and give some direction time and again. And it absolutely means that if somebody is stepping outside of the parameters or protocols, you have to step in and redirect.

Keep in mind also that through failings you can learn extensively. Some of the greatest learning that ever takes place is through failure. Don't allow your student to fail unsafely or compromise patient care in the name of allowing the student to fail. But you can allow the student to fail and maintain respect so that they remember or learn from those mistakes. It's much more impressionable to understand the learning after failure has taken place. To simply tell somebody what to do and when to do it is not as effective is allowing them to do it themselves. This is very difficult for you as preceptor. You're being asked to balance allowing somebody the latitude of developing and implementing their own plans and, in the same way, making sure that patient care is not compromised. But this is why you're the preceptor.

And let's remember some of the essential qualities that a paramedic must have. Let's remember the essential qualities of decision-making, consistency, and your methodical approach toward patient care. These are essential qualities of a good paramedic. If you as a preceptor have not mastered these qualities yourself, how are you going to instill them in someone else? These are important questions you have to ask yourself. Are you ready to take on the task of allowing somebody else to take care of your patients? Are you ready for the challenge?

One final note. Being a preceptor is extremely satisfying. When you see how far your student has come since they began with you, you can feel humbled. It's exciting to see others succeed. It's even more exciting to be a part of their success. If you think other people don't ask who you went through your paramedic rides with or who you did your precepting with, you're fooling yourself. Take a sense of pride in the final product and success of your preceptee.

Expectations

Expectations are extremely important. Before a preceptor can even begin precepting, a set standard of expectations has been clearly defined. Determining the expectations begins before your student or your new paramedic arrives at your fire station or ambulance. The expectations begin before the student comes to work with you. You have to determine what the expectations that you have for your student are, before your first interaction. This isn't something that you make up on the fly. You have to have a set standard so that you understand what the goals and objectives need to be. These expectations are tricky sometimes. You have to be honest with yourself, and they have to be reasonable.

Keep in mind that the expectations can work both ways. The expectations that you have for your new paramedic must be developed, but you can also have expectations for yourself. It's always good to have goals that you yourself are working toward. As a new preceptor or even an experienced one, having expectations of yourself is extremely important. This is the time to reflect on what those expectations for you could be.

Now moving on toward the expectations of your new paramedic or student. These expectations are extremely important as well. First, you have to begin with setting the standard of a good work ethic within the organization, and then you have to present your expectations to the new paramedic. It's difficult to hold somebody to a standard when that standard has not been defined. This is the importance of the expectations. We often become frustrated or upset with people—and in this case students or new paramedics—because they're not operating in the manner in which we would like to see. However, this is not a reasonable approach to precepting. You can't hold somebody to a standard that has not been defined. You can't become upset with somebody when the expectations haven't been presented. Don't become that instructor who randomly gets upset or frustrated with your preceptee because they're not doing things properly when you haven't even defined what you want.

Some of these expectations should be internalized within the new paramedic or the student—such as work ethic and accountability. However, you may have to elaborate on what you mean when you say we have to have a good work ethic. Maybe it means when we come into work every day your expectations are that the two of you go through your medications and check equipment. Your expectation is that your student shows up on time every day, properly dressed in the proper uniform, and looks presentable to the public.

Now before continuing with your expectations of your new preceptee, let's address something first. It's important for you to begin with telling your preceptee what they can expect from you. This is your moment as a preceptor and this is the moment that you will be held to. Your preceptee will hold you to these statements and the information that you tell them that they can expect from you. Do not, however, bail out or take the easy way out and not do this pivotal part. Your preceptee deserves to know and deserves to have it defined what they can expect from you, and you have to be willing to live by what you tell them. You have to hold yourself accountable.

These are all aspects of the relationship that make the internship or the field instruction process easier because now the student or the new paramedic has a framework by which they can begin to assimilate into your world of precepting. They now have a foundation by which they can begin to move and navigate because they know what they can expect from you. This is an extremely important aspect to the expectations. This also is arguably the most difficult task as a preceptor to do. Because now all of a sudden you're putting your word and actions on the line. You're not only going to tell them what your expectations of them are, but you're going to have to be accountable also. This goes back to the attributes of professionalism, accountability, and integrity. You have to let them know what to expect and you have to hold yourself to it.

Remember we were talking about how expectations work both ways? Expectations are not merely your requirements of the student or new paramedic; expectations work in both ways. You must allow the student to articulate the expectations they have for you. This is not unreasonable that the new student has expectations for the preceptor. It's no different than when you yourself were in paramedic school trying to learn a new skill or concept. You had expectations that you would learn these things and that those instructors would teach them to you. It's no different here. You now have become the preceptor, and the expectation of your preceptee is extremely important.

Now we all know that ultimately their goal or their expectation is that you will instruct them properly, teach them the ways of being a good paramedic, and pass them and let them go off on their own (and be continued in their world of paramedicine). They may have more specific expectations that need to be dealt with in the immediate internship or field instruction. Allowing your new paramedic to articulate expectations of you does multiple things.

First and most importantly, it opens the door for communication. Immediately your preceptee understands that their voice will be heard and that they have a forum in which to speak and express themselves and their own concerns. The mastery of your skill as a preceptor comes into play once again. Here is where you have to listen to what the student has to say because they will have an understanding of some of their deficiencies. They will also have an understanding of their strengths. Allow them to tell you what those strengths are and what those weaknesses are. Allow them the opportunity to tell you what their concerns are and what they're nervous about and if and why they're anxious about the new role they are stepping into.

Allow them to speak without judgment. Keep in mind that anxiety about the new role doesn't necessarily mean they are deficient or unable to perform; it simply means that they're taking on a new role that they should be concerned about. Healthy anxiety can be an attitude that you as a preceptor can absolutely make into a good thing. Communication is integral to precepting.

Allowing the student to articulate their expectations also makes your job easier because now you can begin to have a framework or formulate a plan by which to instruct them. If they come to you and they know that they lack skills in specific areas or knowledge base in specific areas, now you can really begin to formulate your plan for teaching and mentoring them. Allowing them to express themselves and their concerns and their expectations for you is extremely critical to their own success, and your success as an instructor.

Now we can move forward to the learning environment. Remember that expectations are critical, and they set the foundation for the learning environment you want to create.

Learning Environment

We've discussed the importance of expectations—both the expectations of you as the preceptor and the expectations of your preceptee. This comfortably leads us into the whole purpose of the internship or the field instruction process in the first place, and that is the learning environment. What makes an effective learning environment? How do you establish a good learning environment? After all, that's the entire purpose of your being a preceptor, to mold the new paramedic.

The learning environment begins with communication, which starts by you discussing and articulating expectations. You're already some of the way there if you've addressed the expectations. You've begun to open up the doors for communication and thus started the process of creating your learning environment. By following these principles you have created an environment in which there are no hidden agendas; unknowns no longer exist. Your student will have no questions about what the expectations are and have no anxiety about coming to you and communicating with you. The anxiety that the new student or the new paramedic has is already going to be evident. You have to do what you can to eliminate other processes and activities that are going to be cause for further anxiety. By creating the proper learning environment, you can do that.

Keep in mind your students' anxiety will help you as a preceptor create a better learning environment. Keep your student or preceptee involved in all the processes. Make sure that they're well informed and you're continually communicating with them on what you're seeing, wanting, or doing. By opening up these doors of communication, you also take away the anxiety that your student will have with speaking to you personally, as the preceptor. You shouldn't have an environment that you've created in which your student or preceptee doesn't want to talk to you about problems or concerns. That is not a proper learning environment, and learning will not take place.

We also need to discuss the importance of honesty. We've gone over integrity and honesty in depth and have addressed it as a key characteristic or attribute that a successful paramedic must have. But it's also incredibly important for the preceptor. You have to be honest with your preceptee in order to create a successful learning environment. If your preceptee does not trust you, they're not going to ask you questions, and, again, learning is not going to take place.

If your preceptee is asking you questions that you don't know the answer to, be honest with them and let them know that you don't know the answer. Now those questions you don't know the answer to are important to remember, so you better write them down and make them a priority. Those questions are important, and they also contribute to the learning environment because it demonstrates to the preceptee that their concerns are being addressed by you, and are important to you. Do not get caught lying or trying to weasel your way out of addressing questions with your preceptee. Don't minimize their ability to analyze truth. You don't want to be caught lying to them. The learning process will immediately stop.

The learning environment continues in the importance of assimilation. A brief note: For some reason people sometimes think that you must be "hard," so to speak, on somebody in order to make them better. This is not the case. You should set forth reasonable expectations and reasonable goals that they must achieve in order to make them better. To be arbitrarily or unjustly hard on somebody is an improper approach to developing a paramedic, a person, and especially a learning environment. Don't require abstract goals from your preceptee without having a purpose in mind. You shouldn't arbitrarily have your student do tasks in order to do them and be "hard" on them. There should be intent and purpose behind what you're doing and what you're asking them to do. Your intentions also need to be clearly communicated to your student.

You must allow them to assimilate into the team. Many of you are going to work in different environments, whether it's a paramedic on an ambulance with an EMT or another paramedic. You might be on a fire department and you've got to bring this new student or preceptee into the fire station with your entire crew. The point is that the preceptee needs to be allowed to assimilate and feel like part of the team. If you keep the student at a distance, they will remain there. It's your responsibility to bring them in and create the environment that they can assimilate and feel as if they're part of the team. By allowing this to happen, you've created more open lines of communication, which goes back to the learning environment.

With your student or your preceptee assimilated into the group or into your team, they are comfortable communicating with the other team members about what they are seeing, what they want, what needs to be done, and what they're trying to accomplish. There will no longer be any hesitation on their part because they're comfortable and they feel as if they're part of the team. This is an extremely important aspect to developing and creating a proper learning environment.

We briefly mentioned this but will reiterate just how important this principle of assimilation is. Without allowing your student to assimilate into the team, all you've done is keep them at a distance, hindering their learning. They may actually appear as though they are answering your questions and doing what you're requiring of them, but in reality they're not addressing their personal needs or their personal concerns. They're just addressing what you require of them and appeasing whatever sort of expectation you have. This is a dangerous situation for a learning environment because they're not learning how to be a proper paramedic and good decision-maker. Instead, they're learning what your buttons are and how to properly appease you. This is not the definition of a proper learning environment. If you don't allow your student to assimilate into the team, this is what will happen.

Continuing with the lines of a learning environment and communication, we must address the student and your comfort level. You now as the preceptor are going to be required to remain cool, have your emotions in check, and not become overly agitated or extremely frustrated. It is now your job to remain calm and decent when speaking with your preceptee or your student. Do not talk *at* your student. We all know exactly what we're talking about. Nobody likes to be spoken at. Simply put, this is condescending. Don't be condescending to your student, it is disrespectful. We like to be informed, we like to take constructive criticism, we like to be a part of our learning environment and our learning, but we don't like to be spoken at. You don't like it, so don't do it to your student.

Second, do not embarrass your student. If you think that publicly embarrassing your student because of a misstep in front of the crew, in front of the ambulance crew, in front of the police department, in front of the hospital, you are wrong. Do not publicly embarrass your student because they will absolutely shut down. Learning will no longer take place because you have sabotaged their trust. They will no longer confide in you and no longer trust what you have to say because you've embarrassed them. And you should understand that this is a natural response to being embarrassed. It will completely inhibit the learning process and is inappropriate to do to your student.

You cannot compromise patient care. This is in the immediate sense. If something is going on that needs to be addressed for some safety reason or a patient care reason, then address it professionally. However, to openly and publicly embarrass your student for the sole purpose of demonstrating your superior knowledge or ability is absolutely inappropriate, not to mention unprofessional. Don't necessarily feel as if you have to address every single situation and everything that happens on a scene publicly. However, if there are patient care problems that need to be addressed, you should absolutely address them. Addressing a treatment plan or deviating from your student's treatment plan because it is in your patient's best interest must be done so professionally. This is why you are the preceptor in the first place. You must be confident that you can rein in any problems that manifest. You will notice that this is easily done, and your student will not even know until afterward in many cases, if you do it professionally and skillfully.

Moving forward, we also must keep in mind that we cannot disrespect our students or preceptees. Don't disrespect them by attacking them personally. Don't disrespect them publicly, and don't disrespect them privately. This is a professional environment and professional world. Your emotional response to situations should not elicit a personal attack on somebody or their person. Be careful not to disrespect somebody because it will absolutely stop the learning environment.

This isn't to say that certain issues don't need to be addressed. If somebody is being unprofessional or lacks integrity or if a student is not being honest or is lacking in any of the other qualities we've discussed, you need to address the situation. This must be done in a professional way and not a personal one. Your job as the preceptor is to mold the paramedic in a professional world. Don't allow your emotions to overcome you and dictate how you treat people in a professional world. If we as emergency responders want the public to treat us professionally, we must first start by treating each other professionally.

Treat everyone professionally, treat them decently, treat them with respect, treat them with the dignity they deserve. If you're decent and reasonable to your preceptees, they will respond favorably and you have developed a learning environment.

Don't require something from a student that you yourself are not willing to do. This is not creating a proper learning environment. Additionally, it's important to understand your individual student. Don't push them beyond their capacity. Some students learn more quickly and develop faster. Some students take longer to develop, take a longer internship or a longer field instruction process, and that's okay. However, that's your job as the preceptor to determine how they're coming along, what they need to work on, or if they need additional time. These things are important and the preceptee must be given the time needed to develop and demonstrate growth and decision-making.

You can push them to be better (but not too hard) and motivate them by giving them goals and objectives that they need to reach. They should be coming into the internship every day with a specific goal in mind that they want to accomplish, and that you've required of them. Just don't make it unreasonable. It is unprofessional for you to create an environment in which you know the student will fail at the task that you are setting forth. Don't set people up for failure. Creating goals and expectations in this fashion must be done case by case. Provide opportunities for success in each expectation and goal you have set forth.

Let's address something else that makes a proper learning environment. That is sensitivity. You as the preceptor are now the leader, you're the mentor, you are the one who will be looked up to. You will set the tone for all activities. You have to be sensitive to both the student's anxiety and the student's life. You must be sensitive to extenuating circumstances—the factors that are beyond anybody's control that may impact the student's ability to perform—for example, a death in the family.

This isn't to say that they are not still going to be required to perform, but be sensitive to it. Maybe pushing somebody every single day and requiring jobs of them every single day is not the best practice for your specific student. You have to be sensitive to worldly events that are going on in your students' lives that may impact their work. For instance, what if your student has an immediate change in their childcare? Childcare is a realistic need that must be addressed. The student or preceptee cannot be expected to perform properly if they are concerned about their children.

Don't brush this off as though they need to leave their home life at home, come to work, and have no relationship with what's going on in their personal lives. That's completely unreasonable and improper. We're not developing people who compartmentalize their lives to such a degree that they have no ability to make life decisions while at work because they're so consumed with exactly what's happening at work. Be sensitive to your students' needs outside of work.

Ah, but that's a thin line. You have to be able to discern what is important personally and what is not. You have to be willing to step in and the student has to understand that they are in an internship. This is a rigorous and selective process. They must have the understanding that it is going to be difficult. They are going to be required to be front and center for the duration, and they must be engaged. However, understanding and being sensitive to worldly things that are outside of everybody's control will create a better learning environment. They will trust you more and you will have gained their respect. Now they will even more easily, and confidently, come to you with problems that they have or concerns that they feel need to be addressed.

So now we come to the part where you understand or you should understand that you are the leader. You're now assuming an entirely different role than just practicing your own medicine. The learning process and developing the learning environment is the most important part of teaching somebody. If students are not comfortable in the environment that you've created, they will not learn, much less realize their own potential. Now it's up to you as the leader to create that environment. It's now up to you to develop the paramedic. To develop an environment in which they feel comfortable enough to learn. You are now the professional mentor, so act like it. Be the preceptor that the student needs and wants.

Evaluations

The evaluation process for a preceptor is ongoing. The first part of evaluation should almost go without being said. However, it seems as though some preceptors need to be reminded that in order to actually precept, you have to be present. We can't tell you how many times we've personally witnessed preceptors in charge of educating and directing new paramedics, but they are not even present in the room when the patient assessment is going on. We've walked out of rooms before and seen the preceptor standing outside and not even paying any attention to what their student or paramedic trainee is even doing. Which seems that sometimes preceptors take the role of preceptorship and commit it to being a free pass. They almost present themselves as if it's a free workday—when in contrast it should be an even more difficult workday.

The reality is that being a preceptor demands that you are ever vigilant about what's actually going on with your preceptee. How can you identify conditions if you're not even willing to stand in the room and observe what's actually taking place?

Again, this should be obvious, but being a preceptor is a huge responsibility. This isn't the time to consider yourself off for the day because you have somebody else to do the reports or ask the questions or develop the treatment plans or whatever the case may be. This is the time to mold the new medic. This is the time that you have to take extra consideration into developing treatment plans, go into the minutiae and the minute details of why somebody's doing what they're doing. You have to be present and observe what students are doing in order to actually evaluate their skills.

Don't take the preceptor role as lackadaisical or turn off your own willingness to practice medicine. Don't just consider yourself a third rider, so to speak, and now all of a sudden you have somebody who's going to do all the work for you and all you have to do is educate them on specifics or whatever comes up. This isn't the time to sit back and relax. This is the time to become more involved in every aspect of patient care.

Before even setting foot in the role of being a preceptor, you have to commit to a certain degree or willingness to provide ongoing evaluation. You can't simply come in and take a snapshot in time of something that you've seen or heard, or something that your student has done and make gross or general judgments or evaluations based off that single snapshot. This is an ongoing commitment to ongoing learning and evaluation. You have to understand that you are now being asked to commit a certain degree of time and energy to developing somebody in their new role as a paramedic. You must be committed to an ongoing evaluation.

So how does the evaluation process begin? We've stated that you have to be present and observing what is actually taking place in order to evaluate. We've also mentioned that it is important to have a commitment to ongoing evaluation. What is the evaluation process? How do you actually evaluate somebody? How do you begin?

The most important process of the evaluation is the initial evaluation. Similar to your initial assessment when you respond to an alarm or begin to address patient care, you need to create an initial evaluation. How do you create an initial evaluation? It's not based on what you've heard about the new paramedic or how you've worked with them in the past as an EMT. Those factors may play minor roles in how you're going to develop an evaluation plan for them. However, it's not fair to evaluate somebody that you haven't observed practicing yet. The initial evaluation is extremely important.

You must allow a certain amount of time in order to evaluate them working and observe them working in the new capacity. You have to observe them practicing medicine and assessing patients. You have to observe their skills, their patient interactions, their interpersonal skills, and their mechanical skills. You have to observe their report writing, treatment plans, and approach toward situations. You have to observe all the actions that are present in taking care of a patient. Once you've observed these activities for a period of time, then you can evaluate and assess what needs to be addressed.

You can't just go into evaluating a new paramedic without actually, silently evaluating how they work. You have no foundation on which to evaluate if you haven't observed them working in that capacity yet. Keep in mind that you are allowing them leeway to practice, which goes back to your need as a preceptor to be a master of adaptation. You have to allow them to practice the medicine the way they want to practice.

You can't mold somebody if you don't even know which direction you need to take them. There may be skills that they're extremely good at. You must be willing to observe them in order to see where you have to go next. This initial observation time is not set in stone. It doesn't have to be a set amount of time, but you just have to make sure that you have a good foundation or understanding of what the new paramedic needs in order to progress.

This could be anywhere from a single call to a couple of calls, to a couple of days. If you allow them to run that initial call to observe them, and there are obvious problems that need to be addressed, then clearly you can begin to address them. You've already begun to evaluate them by observing these tasks that need to be addressed, but now you can develop a plan to address them properly.

This is where the preceptor's expertise comes into play and is extremely pivotal. This is where your expertise is needed, and your communication skills are crucial and integral. You have to be able to determine what is grossly lacking. You have to determine what good habits are already present, what needs to be addressed immediately, and what can wait.

Remember to keep in mind that there may be certain aspects that have to be addressed with some people that don't need to be addressed with others. You don't always have to address the same exact points; however, the principles of decision-making, consistency, methodical approach, and these important principles of being a paramedic need to be addressed, but the particular things may not need to be.

So what does a teaching plan look like? How do you develop a teaching plan?

A teaching plan can be extremely simple, or it can be complex. Depending on what is lacking within the new paramedic determines how complex or simple the teaching plan needs to be. Your teaching plan can go from call to call. Your teaching plan can go from day to day. Your teaching plan can go from set to set. But keep in mind that you have to continually evaluate if the goals within the teaching plan are being met to move forward.

An example of a simple teaching plan would be that you want to focus solely on the assessment. This is a simple teaching plan. You just want a new paramedic to go in and assess the patient. Just the assessment, not a treatment plan, not implementing skills, starting IVs, or putting on EKG leads. Some students need to learn how to assess a patient. They just need to talk. That is an example of a simple teaching plan. And then after developing that skill in your student, you can move on to other tasks within the realm of being a professional paramedic.

An example of a complex teaching plan would be putting together an entire scheme for patient care. For instance, you need the student to develop a more global or a bigger picture. You need them to be able to become more proficient at multitasking, so you may ask them to assess a patient while also putting on EKG leads or performing other task-oriented interventions. You might ask them to assess the patient and then, while they're doing that, ask them questions that determine what they're thinking. While they are assessing the patient, start asking them to develop a treatment plan and about how they're going to implement it, what strategies they're going to use to extricate the patient from the situation or transport priorities.

Teaching plans also need to be developed with the new paramedic—in cooperation with them. Now obviously you as the preceptor are the expert; however, their input is important because they have to be vested in the plan to become better at it. Or to properly reach the targeted goals or the desired goals. They also have to be involved to properly understand what those goals are so that they can meet them. It's much easier to implement a teaching plan with the student involved if they are invested in the plan itself. It's easier if they understand what is actually being asked of them if they're involved in developing the actual teaching plan.

If you need to address a skill issue with the student, you might ask them how they want to go about addressing the skill. If they're not good at IVs, you can ask them what they need and how you could help them. Maybe their concern has nothing to do with actually doing anything on calls but going over and addressing simple techniques. Now obviously you would have to start IVs to become proficient, but beginning with some simple instruction and technique critiques in the station or in the back of the ambulance while waiting for an alarm is helpful. Make sure you involve them in all aspects of their preceptorship, which also includes the teaching and evaluation process. They will be invested in the process if they are more involved.

Another important aspect of the initial evaluation is getting the best out of your time with them. Remember you don't have that much time with students. You don't have all the time in the world to critique and make sure that every little detail is perfected. This is where you begin to figure out and prioritize what needs to be addressed first, what needs to be addressed the most, or what's the most lacking in their patient care. This assessment allows you to not waste time on skills that are already present.

Some students are excellent at talking to strangers. Some are terrible at talking to strangers. This would be a simple example of needing to create different teaching plans for different students based on their needs. Don't waste your time making the person who is excellent at talking to strangers focus on those skills. Conversely, the student who is unable to talk to strangers is going to have to work excessively at assessing patients, at talking to strangers, at basic communication skills. Use the time as efficiently as you can.

Take the time to reinforce the good habits, skill sets, and behaviors that your student already has. When they are utilized, quickly reinforce that they did a good job and make sure they are getting positive feedback. This is critical to the evaluation. When your student is encouraged, it will drive them toward success. You might say, "That was a textbook intubation." "Great job on securing the airway, perfect technique, bro."

Now you'll implement the teaching plan that you have devised with your student or new paramedic. You have to implement it and observe how they are developing. You have to set benchmarks within the plan that the student or new paramedic should be making. Those benchmarks are important so that you can create a more global picture of what the goal is. Once they hit those benchmarks, then you can move past them. This is important in your ongoing evaluation of the student.

You have to be able to revisit the teaching plan and evaluate whether or not those benchmarks are being met. You have to evaluate whether the desired results are being met. This also goes back to keeping the student informed and involved in the process. This can only happen if you clearly communicate your expectations for them, and determine how you are going to evaluate.

Keep in mind that the evaluation process is extremely fluid. You may implement teaching plans and think that you've got everything figured out, and then through a period of observation realize that your true focus needs to be elsewhere. This is okay. You have to be able to adjust accordingly to what your student needs. While you work more and more with the student or the new paramedic, you will begin to understand what their needs are more definitively.

This flexibility is why it is important to develop trust with your trainee. You have to invest time and effort with them.

This will be clearly demonstrated to your trainee, and they will respond appropriately.

Don't get discouraged if you have to redirect or adjust a teaching plan or implement an entirely new teaching plan during the process of precepting. You just have to be able to adjust in view of that need. Don't become so fixated on one specific goal that you think is so important that you overlook other aspects to the patient care that need to be addressed.

What we have learned is that if you implement this type of philosophy of training with your student, it is inevitable that you will change your teaching plan. You will have to adjust it because at some point in the process your student has a light-bulb go on. They realize you are teaching them the art of caring for people, professionalism, and decision-making—and not how to perform interventions. Their growth and development begin to expand so rapidly that you now get to sit back and enjoy the ride. You adjust your teaching plan to mentor their thoughts and ideas about situations rather than their need for specific interventions. It is an incredibly humbling and fulfilling experience to watch a student of yours perform and grow so quickly.

If you start to realize that there are other aspects that need to be addressed, begin addressing them. If the student is not ready to move forward from simple to complex teaching plans, you may need to ask for more time with the student, or you may need to send them back for some additional training.

You have to be able to implement multiple teaching plans sometimes. You may have to implement teaching plans that involve specific skills or communication or transport priorities or differential diagnoses. You can develop a number of teaching plans, but you may have to implement multiple teaching plans at the same time. Just keep in mind that the goals need to be communicated clearly.

How do you measure a trainee's ultimate success? Here are four principles that we routinely use to evaluate if someone is now capable of operating independently as a paramedic:

1. A continued demonstration of medical principles that were learned in paramedic school (such as cardiology, pharmacology). Also a demonstration of proficiency in skills needed as a paramedic (in other words, starting IVs and intubation). And if applicable a demonstration of working knowledge of your system's guidelines or protocols.
2. An ability to comfortably and appropriately change treatment plans on the fly during a critical call. This should be done independently of your prompt that a change needs to happen.
3. In virtually everyone that we have trained there comes a point at which the trainee is no longer discussing treatment plans and differentials with the instructor as a student. They are interacting with you as the instructor on a peer-to-peer basis, instead of on a student-instructor basis. That transition is telling you that they are becoming comfortable with administering treatment plans independent from your input. Keep in mind that this should only come after lots of training and interacting with you as an instructor. Your constant mentorship has now given them the confidence to work as a paramedic. They are now demonstrating to you that they can appropriately treat someone with their own decision-making process.
4. This one is perhaps the most important. Your student must demonstrate a willingness to take responsibility for their actions. Are they willing to be held accountable for the decisions that they make? This is

vital. What this shows is that the trainee completely understands the implications of their actions or lack of action and is willing to take responsibility for it. It also shows that they are confidently making decisions because they know they won't make excuses, and they own the decisions they make.

9

Putting It All Together

Having Fun

Studies and statistics might support the idea that while having fun at work you are more productive. We would also argue that this profession of ours incorporates high levels of stress, high levels of anxiety, and a high degree of difficulty. However, it is also a profession that is unique in character and can generate high levels of enjoyment and job satisfaction. Whether or not we can support those statements with studies is irrelevant. We and those we have worked with closely can attest to those facts. This brings us to another important principle while precepting a new paramedic: Have fun.

Responders develop the idea that everything has to be full-tilt serious 100 percent of the time. We don't understand that philosophy. This job is stressful and has enough anxiety as it is. So let's have some fun! Have a laugh or two and enjoy yourself. Why is it that we create this unrealistic idea of perfection

100 percent of the time? That is incredibly unreasonable and just adds to your stress. Having fun with the greatest job there is—absolutely essential. And it's also incredibly important to the learning process. Those who learn in an environment that is fun and enjoyable learn much more.

This job is the greatest. People are lined up around the corner for your job. There are people begging to get on a fire department. Some try numerous times and put in multiple applications to land your job. Applicants are signing up to be EMTs and paramedics everywhere you go. You have a great job. You also have a fun job. You have a job that allows you to interact with people on an extremely personal basis and in an exceptionally vulnerable time in their lives. This job is difficult and has high levels of responsibility, but it also carries with it a uniqueness in work. You must have fun. You must be able to display this with your preceptee.

Do you remember when you were a green, brand new EMT and you got your first IV on a real patient? How exhilarating, how fun, how satisfying. We all remember the first time we successfully intubated a patient in the field, on a real call. We remember the exhilaration and the satisfaction and the enjoyment because of a job well done. We continue to have enjoyment in a job well done.

One of the most important steps of education and precepting as it relates to this job is that of positive reinforcement. Why is there a constant desire to address all the negatives or all of the failures within the internship? "You didn't do this right, you didn't do that right, you need to work on this, you need to work on that." Those criticisms are important in their own time and in their own place. But that can't be the only detail that you're continually addressing. You must adopt an attitude of positive reinforcement. Positive reinforcement adds to the fun of the job. Try it. Go on, try it. Take a shift and force yourself to positively reinforce all the great tasks your preceptee does. It'll be fun.

Positive reinforcement is a reflection of your devotion to your student's success. You must become involved in the learning of your student. It must become important to you as a preceptor to see them succeed. This is not a process by which you're trying to help somebody fail. This is a process in which you're trying to help them succeed. Having fun is absolutely necessary for your preceptee's ultimate success.

When your student goes in and gets a successful IV, that right there should be reinforced. You should be excited about their successes. You should reinforce and instill an attitude of excitement and enjoyment and fun when it comes to them doing a job well done. If that manifests with you saying "great tube" or "awesome line," that's great. It's up to you how to communicate this to your preceptee. Those are important words that your student wants to hear and needs to hear. We all like to be in a position where we're told we are doing well and meeting the expectations.

[Chris's story] I remember doing a firefighting hoseline evolution. I was a brand new firefighter, and we had to do a flowing 2 1/2-inch nozzle class. For those that don't know, flowing a fire attack line can be exhausting. We had to flow a 2 1/2 while advancing through a hallway in order to extinguish a fire. I remember that was some of the hardest, most physically exhausting work I have done. But I also remember my instructor when I was done came running down the hallway and gave me the biggest jump high five in the world. He was utterly ecstatic with how well I had done. He was so happy to see me work hard, to see I successfully finished the evolution. I was thrilled to see him excited for me that it made me want to do better. It's imperative that you create that same environment for your students.

It's crucial for you to be invested in their learning so that you become excited for them; in turn, they will become more motivated to do better and better. When you reinforce their successes, they become more successful. They then become better with their ability, and the desire to learn just grows. We have enough to worry about in this job, we have enough responsibilities, we have enough burdens, and we have enough guidelines and principles that we must follow and adhere to strictly. You must have a willingness and an ability to have fun with the successes that you experience.

Now, we feel as though we have to qualify the statements of having fun while working in this profession. Unfortunately, some will take what we've said about having fun and misunderstand or misinterpret. The intensity that goes along with being a paramedic is not something that has to be evident and expressed all the time. There needs to be enjoyment in your job. That needs to be passed on to your preceptee.

Don't misunderstand, we are not advocating—and in fact it would be the exact opposite—that you adopt an attitude of less than professionalism. We are simply stating that within the realm of paramedicine, you can actually have fun doing this job and remain a constant, consummate professional. There is no contradiction in practice when it comes to having fun and being a professional. You can be the most intense, consummate professional while still enjoying your job and having fun doing it. These things are important to keep in mind.

When you're having fun with your preceptee and taking joy in all of their successes, that's reflective of your ability to properly instruct them. Having fun during the instruction process makes it more palatable to the student to hear the negative comments that they need to work on. You can't always drudge on about their deficiencies, but always address their successes.

As we develop this thought of having fun while at work, which should be obvious, let's develop it as it relates to your direct patient care. Enjoying your job will immediately be evident with your patients. Your patients will sense whether or not you enjoy what you're doing. We can't tell you how many times we've been told by patients that we're doing a great job simply because of our attitude and nothing to do with actual interventions. Simply because of our enjoyment at work, our ability and willingness to have fun at work while precepting somebody or simply practicing paramedicine.

If you have adopted an attitude where you're no longer having fun being a paramedic, it's time for you to bug out. Maybe you need a break. Vacation? Maybe you need to promote. Maybe you need to get out of the game and move on. There's no shame in that, but there is a level of responsibility that you have to the public and to your patients. If you are going on alarms right now and you're telling yourself, *I wish I didn't have to run another call* or *I wish I didn't have to do this paperwork*, it's time to reevaluate whether you should continue in this profession. Poor attitude will come out and will manifest in poor patient care.

Again, let's qualify these statements. We're not saying that we as paramedics, EMTs, medical providers, or firefighters are having enjoyment in the misfortunes of others. We're not saying that you should be having fun because somebody else is having the worst day of their life. Don't misunderstand. This is a simple concept. Having fun at work and being a professional are two things that can go hand-in-hand. You can do both at the same time. We are not advocating for you as a paramedic to take joy in the misfortunes or the tragedies of others.

If you don't enjoy prehospital medicine, your patient will see it. You will be short with them, you will be quick with them, you will be impatient, you will address matters in an unprofessional way, you will not have the willingness to stay with a patient and address issues properly, because you don't enjoy your job. This is the definition of impatience. You have to enjoy your job in order to properly treat people and take care of their family members. You have to enjoy your job to be a good paramedic. This, as it relates to being a preceptor, is also important because your student must witness you enjoying your job so that they can further the tradition of job satisfaction and enjoyment. They can see the enjoyment of this job while also being a professional and take that forward in their own career.

Key Concepts

Okay, we've addressed lots of specific things that are important to being a preceptor. Now let's put it together. Let's summarize what these key concepts are and the principles that you need to implement to be a successful preceptor and to give your students the best chances for success.

This begins with, you guessed it—your ego. Let's fix that problem first and foremost. If you're egotistical, that needs to change. You have to develop and assume a role of service to your preceptee, so don't be so egotistical that you and your own complex get in the way of teaching others. This is important.

Second, we've discussed the importance of expectations. We've discussed how it is essential for you to require expectations of yourself and of your student. It's important to put everything on the table. Without the expectations, it's difficult to evaluate somebody. It's not fair to your student; it's not fair to you; and you will be a better preceptor and will make a better paramedic out of your student if you have the expectations clearly defined.

Professionalism is a common theme within this work. It's the general way by which you must conduct yourself. You as a preceptor now have assumed an enormous responsibility. With that you must be even more professional. You have to be willing to work at professionalism. Don't take a day off; don't take a call off; and don't take a report off. You have to be the consummate professional, the premier example of professionalism for your student.

We've discussed the importance of evaluating people. If you're not willing to evaluate and determine what is deficient and what is lacking, you shouldn't be a preceptor. The importance of evaluation and developing teaching plans is paramount to being a successful preceptor. You must be willing to constantly evaluate and constantly create and develop teaching plans with your student to properly develop them as paramedics.

Everything that we've discussed relates to your role as a preceptor, but let's quickly summarize what it actually means to be a preceptor. Your preceptorship is not designed to make students regurgitate information they already know. But keep in mind that your primary role is to teach your student how to *apply* the knowledge they've already learned. That is extremely important. You have to be so good at your job because you must become a master of adaptation. You have to be willing to adapt to others and their ways of doing things. That's your role to develop a student's ability to make sound decisions within their new role as a paramedic.

These attributes bring us to the pinnacle of precepting. The learning environment. Keep in mind that the learning environment is the place in which you will mold and develop the new medic. You have to create an environment in which they're comfortable and feel as if they can actually learn. Don't be so strict on them that their learning process stops. The learning environment in and of itself is the most important part of their ability to function and develop and learn new concepts as it relates to their profession.

This directly reflects on you as the preceptor. You are responsible for creating the proper learning environment. If your student is not progressing and is not developing as a paramedic, the first thing you need to go to is the learning environment. Determine whether you've created a situation in which they hesitate or they're not learning because of something that you've done. Don't immediately assume that their lack of progress is because of them. First assume their lack of progress is because of you and something you have done to inhibit the learning environment. The learning environment must be safe and comfortable and one that promotes easy communication between you and your student.

And last, but extremely important, have fun. Don't underestimate the contagiousness of an upbeat and positive attitude. Just enjoy your job and enjoy precepting people. Have fun, enjoy the moments. Enjoy the successes. Enjoy the job. Celebrate all of the good things that you and your student and your crew and your department are doing. Celebrate all of the little wins.

These enjoyment processes will foster a fun environment and an environment in which everybody does better and functions better. Not to mention and arguably most importantly, it will create an environment in which your patient care will be better. Your attitude and enjoyment at work will have a direct impact on your patient care, so make it a positive effect, for the better. Pass that on to your student. Remember this: You as a preceptor set the tone for the internship. Make it a tone full of positive morals and attitude. That's how you'll motivate your students to greatness.

Is My Relief Here?

Finally we come to the end. We understand that many of the principles set forth in this book have been reiterated ad nauseam. This was done intentionally to drive the point home. The point is integration. Everything set forth in this book should be integrated into your own practice. If you embrace the idea of integration and embrace the concepts set forth here, it will affect every aspect of your response to an emergency. It will affect how you provide patient care; it will give you more patience with those patients that test us; it will allow you to make better decisions and will allow those decisions to be more consistent; it will build your teamwork and trust within your organization, and the list goes on and on.

If you integrate your understanding of personal interaction with your personal attributes, decision-making, and your educational knowledge, you will benefit greatly. We understand we did not cover basic medical knowledge that you must know in order to properly treat people and make decisions in the field. To reiterate, that knowledge goes well beyond the scope of this book. Understand that knowledge is one of the foundational principles set forth in this book that you must maintain and strive for. Your knowledge of medical principles will direct all of your decisions. You cannot make decisions without the knowledge needed to inform those decisions.

The point here is that you need more than just knowledge to be successful. You have to integrate these two other concepts of practicing and developing your decision-making, and your personal attributes and interpersonal skills. Take the time to develop all three of these principles and then integrate them into your practice every day. All three of these principles strengthen each other.

We've also covered at length what training someone else should look like. We have given you a template to develop a training process for everyone that you train as a preceptor or an instructor. You should take those tasks seriously, and you should instill in your students a sense of professionalism and confidence. Your student should leave you with the understanding that they can go out by themselves and confidently make decisions.

Before we leave you with some advice, we will develop one more point. Discipline. Discipline is the art of forcing yourself to do certain things. Discipline is the key to this entire book. It's the key to the principles and attributes set forth. You must remain disciplined. You must have an attitude of discipline throughout your entire professional practice. You must be disciplined in every aspect of your job. Whether that's getting up in the morning and working out to putting your equipment on the rig properly to checking out all of your medications in your gearbox. You must be disciplined. By being disciplined, you will naturally progress as a paramedic.

When you practice discipline, it becomes habitual. The decisions that you make become decisions based in a disciplined attitude toward situations. Your decisions are not based in some abstract or emotional approach toward something, but they're made in a disciplined manner. Your ability to interpret information, develop a plan, and implement a plan becomes better with discipline.

When you make decisions based in discipline, they, by default, will be better. When you approach a situation and make a decision with some lackadaisical, arbitrary, nonchalant sort of way with no care for the outcome or personal involvement or investment in what actually happens, your decision has no purpose. You have no intent behind what you're actually doing because you don't care.

But the decision made with discipline is the exact opposite. The decision made with discipline involves all of the characteristics we discussed. It involves a disciplined approach and attitude toward the art of improvement, the art of professionalism, the art of integrity and accountability. When you make a decision based in discipline, these other attributes naturally flow into that decision. The decision is made with intent and with purpose and so, by default, will be a better decision because you have a purpose behind what it is. With everything that is written in this book—for all of the attributes, principles, and ideas in the role of a preceptor—practice discipline. Force yourself to be better every single day.

We would each like to leave you with one piece of advice that we feel is extremely important.

The best advice I [Samuel] can give you is that you must understand your medical director's intent. We've gone over this multiple times. I think that this is the most critical aspect of being able to exercise discernment and work within your specific protocols or guidelines. You must understand the intent of your medical directors. If you do not understand what your medical directors are allowing you to do or what their intention is for specific situations, you will never be able to freely act. You'll be in a constant state of contradiction or of misunderstanding or misinterpretation of what it is that your medical directors want you to do. If this is the case, it is incumbent upon you as the provider to communicate to your medical directors that you do not understand what they want from you. Make sure they have clearly communicated to you what their intent is for you to do in specific situations.

To be more specific the best advice I can give you is to understand the intent of your medical directors when it comes to refusals. Understand exactly what they want when it comes to whether or not a patient is capable of refusing. If you understand your medical directors' intention, that allows you to freely act. Remember that when you take responsibility for your actions, it gives you liberty. Always stay within your guidelines and your protocols and make sure that you are following them appropriately as set forth by your medical directors.

By now you should understand and have a basic working knowledge of the attributes and principles we've set forth in this book. But we've discussed lots of items. I'll [Chris] offer my advice. First, I think that everyone should be treated with dignity and respect and with professionalism at all times. As mentioned in this book you are not intrinsically better than anyone else; you may just be better off. I truly believe this, and I think it is important to understand this statement. My advice is that if you treat people properly, if you treat people the way that you yourself would want to be treated or your family would want to be treated, you're probably doing the right thing.

If you are consistently adopting an attitude of service to the public and service to those that you're called to help and legitimately trying to better their situation, putting aside your own self-interests and trying to help the person to the best of your abilities, I think that's one of the best pieces of advice I can give. Don't become selfish and egotistical. Don't become someone who wants to or wishes to be served. In contrast, develop the attitude of one who wishes to serve others instead of being served. This attitude will carry you great distances in this profession.

Second, my advice is to consume yourself with the attributes of self-reflection. The attitude and principles of integrity, accountability, professionalism, and decision-making should become habitual. These attributes and principles should be developed and remain consistent. But the attribute of self-reflection is something that demands the art of continued self-discipline. You have to be willing to consistently practice self-reflection. In so doing, you will vastly grow. You will always be in the position of trying to learn new skills and trying to adopt new principles and adopting a better approach toward bettering your skills and those of your team.

By practicing self-reflection you will never be left wanting. Because you always notice that there's something else to grow upon or something else to become better at. This in turn will just carry over into every aspect of your confidence, your attitude, and your approach toward others. Self-reflection is the key. You have to be willing to honestly assess yourself and see what you need to improve on.

Don't become burdened by your mistakes. Don't allow your self-reflection to impact you negatively. You must remember that as a paramedic or first responder you can only make the best decision you can with the limited information in front of you. As you reflect, you will catch and see mistakes you make, so learn from them and move on. This should motivate you toward excellence, not cause you to become fearful of action.

In order to begin the art of truly reflecting on yourself, of truly being disciplined about self-reflection, you must sit down and honestly and truthfully articulate and determine why you're here. Once you develop the idea and develop the attitude of what caused you to be in the position you're in now as a paramedic, everything else becomes easier. Once you understand why you became a paramedic or a first responder, then everything else becomes easier. Because now you've got a framework by which to build upon that is tangible and brings purpose to your life and brings purpose to your practice as a paramedic or a first responder. This will in turn develop your professionalism and you will, by default, hold yourself accountable. In your response to patients and your job and your team, you become personally invested in your own professionalism, which is the key to your practice.

We hope this book has encouraged you. Our intention has been to provide you with an integrated understanding to patient care. We encourage you to study and become the smartest, most informed responders in the business, but don't leave out the other skills necessary to be truly effective. The work of our first responders is outstanding. Long hours, lost sleep, and stressful situations—your communities may never understand your sacrifice, but your brothers and sisters in uniform do. Go out that door with intention. Thanks to all of you for your sacrifices.

Acknowledgments

Chris: Let me finish by thanking my awesome wife, Lexi. Her input and advice was just as valuable and important as mine. Her work ethic is truly something to be admired and mimicked. Thanks for all your patience and support throughout this whole process.

Sam: I would like to thank my wife, Amanda. Her patience with me throughout writing this book and her support of me has been amazing. She gave me constant encouragement and advice. Thank you for your support.

About the Authors

Samuel and Christian Adams are identical twin brothers. They have over twenty years of experience responding to 911 calls. They both love working as firefighter/paramedics for the Colorado Springs Fire Department (CSFD), and they fervently believe in providing the highest quality patient care to the citizens of Colorado Springs.

Christian Adams is a Nationally Registered and Colorado State Certified Paramedic. He is also certified in RSI (rapid sequence intubation). In 2012 he was honored as the Pridemark/ Rural Metro Paramedic of the Year for the Denver metro area. He is trained and has worked with the CSFD TEMS (Tactical EMS) team and currently functions as a paramedic with the city's High Angle Rope Rescue team. He also functions as a paramedic preceptor for the CSFD.

Christian has an associate of arts degree from the New Mexico Military Institute and a bachelor's degree in criminal justice from the University of Northern Colorado. When not responding to alarms, his favorite pastime is enjoying the Colorado outdoors with his wife and two boys.

Samuel Adams is a Nationally Registered and Colorado State Certified Paramedic. He is certified through the CSFD for RSI (rapid sequence intubation). He started his EMS career working as an EMT basic in the Denver metro area. After going through paramedic school he worked in the Denver area as a paramedic responding to 911 calls. He is on the CSFD TEMS unit for the city (Tactical EMS). His current assignment is as part of the wildland firefighting deployment team for the Colorado Springs Fire Department.

In 2017 Samuel was named paramedic of the year for the Colorado Springs Fire Department. Sam also serves on a paramedic advisory committee for the CSFD, which advises the EMS system in Colorado Springs. Sam also works as a paramedic preceptor for the CSFD. He has an associate of arts degree from the New Mexico Military Institute and a bachelor's degree in criminal justice from the University of Northern Colorado. His time is best spent with his wife camping in the summers and being around his two brothers.